FEAR AND FASHION IN THE COLD WAR

FEAR AND FASHION IN THE COLD WAR

JANE PAVITT

V&A Publishing

First published by V&A Publishing, 2008
V&A Publishing
Victoria and Albert Museum
South Kensington
London SW7 2RL

Distributed in North America
by Harry N. Abrams, Inc., New York

ISBN 978 1 85177 544 6
Library of Congress Control Number
2008924024

Design: A Practice for Everyday Life
Copy-editor: Delia Gaze

New V&A photography by Christine
Smith, Paul Robins and Ken Jackson,
V&A Photographic Studio

Front cover illustration:
John French, fashion photograph
featured in 'Space Hats' *Daily Mail*
(15 June 1965). Hat by Edward Mann.
V&A: JF6925/8, AAD/1979/9

Back cover illustration:
Space Age styling from Soviet designers:
the Muscovite model Galina Milovskaya
wears a metallic ensemble with a red
fox-fur jacket, leggings and silver boots,
with the Vostok space rocket in the
background, 1968

Printed in Hong Kong by Printing Express

V&A Publishing
Victoria and Albert Museum
South Kensington
London SW7 2RL
www.vam.ac.uk

CONTENTS

INTRODUCTION:

FASHION IN AN AGE OF ANXIETY

FASHION IN AN AGE OF ANXIETY

In the months following the end of the Second World War, the increasing hostilities between the Soviet Union and the United States resulted in much of the world being aligned into two opposing camps. In 1946 Winston Churchill alluded to the presence of an 'Iron Curtain' between East and West Europe.[1] During 1947, as tensions rose over the control and division of Berlin, Europe was effectively divided along Cold War lines. In a poem of that year W. H. Auden described the onset of an 'age of anxiety', in which uncertainty about the future loomed large.[2] The Cold War fired the starting gun on two parallel contests: the arms race and the space race, fostering a culture of suspicion, surveillance and spying, all of which impacted strongly on the art, design, film and literature of the period. Military stand-offs and gestures of defiance, such as the building of the Berlin Wall in 1961 and the Cuban Missile Crisis of 1962, raised tensions to a fever pitch at certain times. The fear of nuclear attack cast a long shadow over the post-war world.

This sense of anxiety coloured many aspects of everyday life, and the conditions of the Cold War influenced a surprising number of cultural products, including designed goods, buildings, films and novels. Yet designers also turned fears into possibilities, finding novelty in the products of a militarized world and assimilating them into a rather hopeful vision of modernity. Despite these concerns, the 1950s and '60s can be characterized as an age of technological utopianism, which invested great faith in the possibility that science could shape the future for the better. For example, glass-reinforced plastic, or fibreglass, used by the military in the production of radar equipment, became a popular material for the manufacture of modern chairs. Innovations adapted for peaceable use, including plastics, computers and microwaves, became part of the landscape of desirable affluence in the post-war Western world. At the cinema, too, fears were turned into pleasures, with popular themes including alien invasion, communist infiltration, spies and the Space Age.

In fashion, Cold War concerns also had their effects. From the bikini to the spacesuit, many forms of attire either sprang from or alluded to Cold War developments. Designed in 1946, the bikini took its name from Bikini Atoll, the Polynesian island location of US nuclear test explosions that year, made soon after the Second World War in Japan had been brought to a sudden end by American bombing of the cities of Hiroshima and Nagasaki with nuclear weapons in 1945. As the world adjusted to the advent of the nuclear age, the 'novelty' of atomic science was nevertheless often invoked as a kind of shock tactic. The French designer Louis Réart, unveiling his microscopic swimwear, declared that it would make an impact of atomic proportions (p.11).[3] In one of the strange contradictions of the Cold War world, the atomic bomb was assimilated into everyday culture as a jaunty symbol of modernity, despite the persistent fear of global annihilation that shadowed the period.

The spacesuit, too, was a product of Cold War aspiration and competition. The Cold War drive to perfect the technologies of global annihilation also resulted in the mission to make man walk on the moon, announced by President J. F. Kennedy in his speech to Congress in 1961, as a counter-attack to the early successes of the

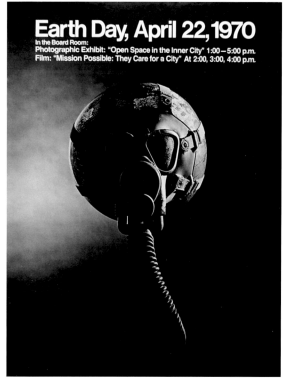

above left:
F.H.K. Henrion, Stop Nuclear Suicide.
Poster for the Campaign for Nuclear
Disarmament, 1963. V&A: E.3910-1983

above right:
Robert Leydenfrost, Earth Day. Poster
promoting environmental awareness-raising
events with a photograph by Don Brewster.
USA, 1970. V&A: E.329-2004

Soviet Union in the Space Race. Emerging from the shadowy world of weapons development in the post-war world, and following the Soviet launch of Sputnik in 1957, the Space Race supplied a new and popular vocabulary of the future. The drive to put a man into space (achieved by the Soviet cosmonaut Yuri Gagarin in 1961), and eventually to walk on the moon (the US *Apollo 11* landing of 1969), created an image of human achievement without parallel (p.15). The Space Race not only provided an enduring stream of technological innovations and material developments that could be adapted to everyday use, but also a host of imaginative possibilities for how products, clothing, environments – even the human body – might be redesigned in the future. No longer was the human body to be limited by its biological capacity for survival on earth.

Paradoxically, in an age lived on the brink of nuclear destruction, the idea of a shiny, happy future made possible by science was enthusiastically embraced. The advancements of the Space Race and the computer age provided the means by which designers could imagine a utopian future, or, alternatively, express their dystopian concerns. The rapid pace of science had altered the relationship between the body and technology, as we shall see in the chapters that follow on the 'Space Age Body' and the 'Cybernetic Body'. The Space Race did more than just fuel a fantasy of a hi-tech future; it also provided new materials with heightened functionality, still familiar to us today, such as Mylar (aluminized nylon), Kevlar and Teflon (both strong and heat-resistant synthetics), and Gore-Tex (a waterproof, breathable fabric). It also accelerated the development of technologies that resulted in many of the personal electronic devices we rely on in the present. Cold War anxieties and hopes prompted an extraordinary range of design proposals for body wear and habitats capable of (or imagined as capable of) supporting life in an uncertain future. Some were utilitarian, such as a plastic decontamination suit made from PVC-coated nylon using high-frequency welding to seal the seams, designed by Frank Hess when a student at the ultra-rationalist Ulm design school (the Hochschule für Gesaltung) in Germany in 1965 (p.12).[4] Others were playful, utopian fantasies, such as Ruben Torres' futuristic menswear of 1967, designed for 'an age of speed, function and leisure'.[5] Commissioned to design men's clothing made from stretch fabric for the in-store boutique of the London store Harrods, Torres proposed figure-hugging one-piece suits without buttons, collars or cuffs, worn with electronic devices on the wrist or belt (p.13).[6] Despite being expressions of the heady optimism of the 1960s, the fashions of the period sometimes reveal a concern to insulate the wearer against the shock of the new, and to equip him or her to deal with the onslaught of information and experience that the modern world had to offer. The youthful and sci-fi mini dresses and knee boots, tunics and jump-suits of the 1960s were frequently accessorized with helmets and visors, balaclavas and armour-plating.

Underpinning the idea of 'future fashion', therefore, were some of the concerns of the age: conflict, nuclear fall-out, pollution, the need for communication and the threat of surveillance. These themes were explored in an exhibition of 1968 entitled *Body Covering* at the Museum of Contemporary Crafts in New York, which emphasized this dual aspect of dress: contrasting fashion as display and spectacle with the role of clothing as protective covering or tool, extending the functioning of the human body. The objects on display included NASA spacesuits, protective clothing (against

Louis Réart (designer), 'Bikini' swimming costume
(in a newsprint-patterned fabric) modelled by dancer
Micheline Bernardini at a beauty contest. Molitor
swimming pool, Paris, 1946

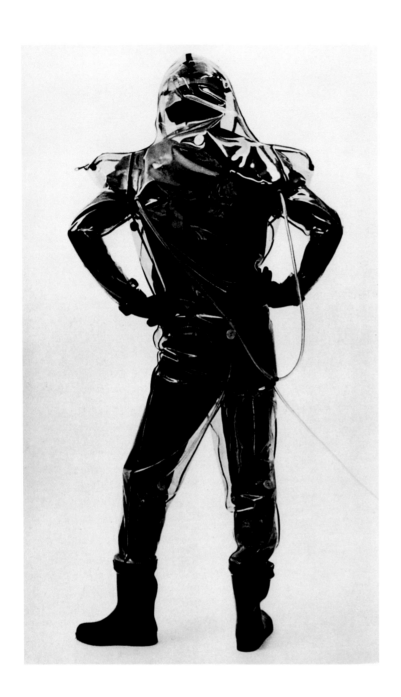

above:
Ruben Torres, sports suit including shoes.
Derendingen fabric with Lycra, 1967

left:
Frank Hess, protective suit, 1965. Student
project at the Hochschule fur Gestaltung.
'Ulm' 19/20, August 1967

above:
Buzz Aldrin and the US flag on the moon.
Photograph. 20 July 1969

left:
Snyder Manufacturing Company, one-piece
air-ventilated protective suit against
radiation, noxious gases and caustic chemicals.
Vinyl film with self-sealing Neoprene zipper,
moulded Polycron boots. 1960s

chemicals and radioactivity), high-performance sportswear, silver mini dresses and avant-garde jewellery. The exhibition catalogue stressed how 'the technological, chemical and electronic knowledge at the disposal of contemporary society makes possible many radical innovations in our concept of body covering'.[7] Many of these innovations were highly speculative; some have become commonplace, such as garments with incorporated electronic devices; whereas others are laughable, such as the idea for the Osmosis Helmet: a 'standard army helmet fitted with a four-inch vertical "mind vibrating engine"'.[8] Nevertheless, the idea of wearable technology (developed from various military conceptions, such as electronic display headgear for pilots) fuelled an alternative vision of mind-expanding artificial experiences, with the body 'plugged in' and 'tuned in' to an electronically enhanced sensory playground.

Against the backdrop of Cold War concerns, *Fear and Fashion* explores the intersection between technology, the body and attire, and how the prevalent anxieties and attendant hopes of the period found their way into fashion. Beginning with the ways in which fashion and the body became sites of Cold War competition, it goes on to explore how the body's vulnerabilities and adaptive capabilities were exploited by scientists and designers, by considering the impact of research into space technologies and cybernetics on clothing, both real and imagined. The book concentrates on the mid-phase of the Cold War in the 1950s and '60s, when technological utopianism, informed by competition between East and West, was perhaps at its height. By the 1970s faith in a scientifically enhanced future was on the decline, and the by-products of Cold War research no longer held the same novelty and appeal for designers.

Introduction

THE COLD WAR BODY

THE COLD WAR BODY

In recent years, fashion historians have become increasingly interested in examining how the confrontations and achievements of the Cold War affected fashion culture. Richly nuanced histories have been drawn from certain clothing types with particular ideological significances, such as the Mao Suit and the Che Guevara T-shirt.[1] Other examples of dress have been used to demonstrate the processes of Cold War cultural exchange and influence: blue jeans, for example, as a symbol of Americanization and youth (and known as *texasky* in Czechoslovakia) took on a particular association when worn by teenagers in the socialist bloc, becoming part of a kind of Cold War mythology of illicit East–West exchange. Studies of socialist fashion cultures have considered the ways in which state fashion institutes in the Eastern bloc attempted to develop forms of 'socialist dress' (which tended to emulate the more modest and conventional styles of Western dressing), as well as considering sartorial sub-cults of the 1950s and '60s, such as the Hungarian *Jampecs* (zoot-suit-wearing rebels) and the Czech *Páseks* (Teddy boys from Prague).[2] Furthermore, intimate histories of personal experience in the Cold War have recently been told through clothing, offsetting the military and political grand narratives of the period. In 2001, for example, an exhibition entitled *Memory of the Body: Underwear of the Communist Era* was staged in St Petersburg and Moscow, in which state-produced utilitarian garments were displayed alongside home-made attempts to copy Western fashions from magazines, exploring the effects of underwear on ideas of the 'Soviet' body.

This chapter explores how both sides in the Cold War negotiated the subject of fashion in the 1950s and '60s, in particular in relation to rivalrous statements regarding cultural superiority and standards of living. It goes on to consider how scientific advancements in materials were deployed as part of the modernizing and competitive rhetoric of both sides. By investing clothing with the same technological progressiveness that was found in the fields of space research, telecommunications and electronics, the fashionable body formed part of the utopian projections of the period. Compare two fashion photographs taken in London in the late 1960s: a fashion shot for *Vogue* and a promotional shot for an exhibition of Soviet achievements held at Earls Court. In the former, the American designer Rudi Gernreich's model and muse Peggy Moffitt is shown wearing his futuristic swimwear in front of the Post Office Tower, a symbol of Britain's 'white heat of technology', the phrase used by Prime Minister Harold Wilson in 1963.[3] Wilson's phrase was continually evoked throughout the decade in order to show faith in a vision of a rapidly modernizing Britain. This kind of juxtaposition was not only confined to the West, as the latter photograph shows. At the Earls Court exhibition, the Russian model in the photograph – wearing a 'nylon one-piece suit with fur cape' – poses in front of a Vostok space capsule, a model of the craft that had first taken Yuri Gagarin into space (p.22).

Rudi Gernreich, swimsuit, lavender wool-knit
top, in front of the Post Office Tower,
London. Photograph by William Claxton, 1960s

Fashion model Mila Romanovkeaja wearing a
nylon one-piece suit with fur cape. <u>Russian
Trade and Industrial Exhibition</u>, Earls Court
Exhibition Centre, London, 1968

COMPETITION

In the post-war period, the spheres of the arts, leisure and domesticity were employed as arenas of Cold War conflict or competition. Sporting events, such as the Olympics, displays of goods at international expos and trade fairs, and touring ballet productions were all, at various times, the subject of rivalrous displays of superiority.[4] One of the central cultural battlegrounds of the 1950s and '60s was the home, since both sides put forward images of domestic modernity. The kitchen, for example, became characterized as a site of competition, as demonstrated in the infamous 'Kitchen Debate' of 1959.[5] Here, at an exhibition in Moscow organized by the United States Information Agency (USIA) to promote aspects of American modernity from streamlined cars to appliance-filled homes, the Soviet Premier Nikita Khrushchev and Vice-President Richard Nixon argued that each rival ideological system could assert its superiority through standards of living. Nixon challenged Khrushchev: 'Would it not be better to compete in the relative merits of washing machines than in the strength of rockets? Is this the kind of competition you want?' (p.25).[6]

Perhaps not surprisingly (and even as the debates shifted throughout the period), fashion was regularly highlighted as an area of ideological difference. The image of material abundance was used, sometimes in an antagonistic manner, to project an idea of the 'good life' in America to the rest of the world. Dress was a means by which two opposing ideological systems could be contrasted – the 'dowdiness' of Russian women, for example, was contrasted in the US press with images of American glamour and elegance. Fashion was also the subject of a moralistic discourse, often cast in Cold War terms. Debates in the East concerned with appropriate forms of 'socialist' dress attacked the sartorial codes of the West. Finally, the relationship between fashion and youth culture, a subject of furious debates on both sides, had particular meaning in terms of their connotations with freedom (in the sense of freedom of self-expression), for example, the wearing of jeans and the expression of sexual freedom through clothing.

In the USSR, the rationing, control and centralization of dress continued after 1945 under systems already in place before the Second World War. Under Stalin, attempts were made to disassociate fashion from its connection with Western, bourgeois values. In the socialist states of Eastern Europe after 1948, the textile and clothing industries were nationalized; private enterprise was prohibited; and discussion centred on how to produce clothing to meet the needs of socialism (p.24). 'Is it possible to strive for a fashion style in harmony with the aims of a socialist state?', enquired one writer in the Czech magazine *Tvar* in 1948. The answer, he asserted, was to design clothing with the same mentality as the architects of the 'new' social housing: to stress practicality and functionality, lack of adornment, purity of shape and character of material.[7]

Even the language of fashion had to change: 'the manner of clothing in the capitalist sphere is aimed at costliness', argued another Czech magazine in 1949.

Dva modely pro ženy KSČ, které
navrhly soudružky z OP Prostějova
jako dar k IX. sjezdu Komunistické
strany Československa. Další modely
najdete uvnitř listu na stránce 14-15.

308

Ročník
Číslo 6
Červen 1949
Cena Kčs 15

Žena
A MÓDA

Cover of <u>Žena a móda</u> (June 1949). Czechoslovakia

*The word elegance, which originally meant gentility, refinement, good
taste, is often used there [in the West] where material, production time
and costly ornamentation are excessive. Thus we are unable to use the
word elegant for suitable and worthy garments … It would seem that,
in the future, it will no longer be desirable to have an elegant suit, to
be elegant. No doubt, we shall substitute this expression with pleasant,
good, smart, tasteful clothing. Those will be the main terms for our clothing
of the future.[8]*

These discussions of dress took a substantial turn in the period following Stalin's
death in 1953, during the years of the so-called Khrushchev Thaw, when Khrushchev
initiated an 'opening up' of the Soviet Union to the West in the interests of 'peaceful
coexistence'.[9] After 1956 magazines could report on Western fashions; new fashion
stores opened; and regular state fashion and trade shows were held as part of the
attempts to create a socialist counterpart to Western consumer capitalism.[10]

Vice-President Richard M. Nixon on a visit to the USSR
shown with Soviet Premier Nikita Khrushchev during the
'Kitchen Debate', 24 July 1959, at the American National
Exhibition, Sokolniki Park, Moscow

LIFE

COLOR: THE MOSCOW FAIR
NIXON ON THE STUMP IN RUSSIA

FAR OUT AND WAY UP:
FAD FOR SPORT PARACHUTING

MMES. MIKOYAN, NIXON
KHRUSHCHEV AND KOZLOV

AUGUST 10, 1959

left:
Cover of Life magazine (10 August 1959),
showing Pat Nixon (centre left) and
Elena Khrushchev (centre right)

below:
'Coiffures Americana' demonstration
in the Beauty Kiosk, American National
Exhibition, Moscow, 1959

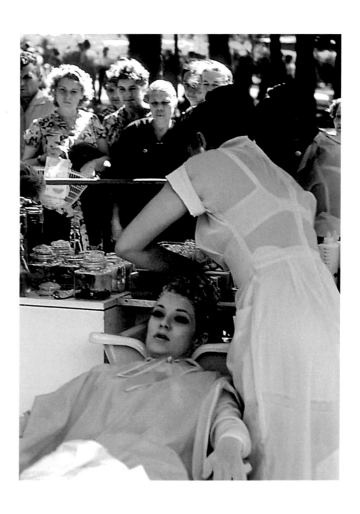

In fact, the forms of official socialist fashion that did emerge did little more than emulate a conventional form of Western 'good taste' dressing, as Djurdja Bartlett has shown.[11] Although it became acceptable to follow the lead of Western design, socialist fashion institutes stressed practicality (given their limited material resources) and the 'moderate' over the 'extreme' in terms of style, whilst the textile and garment industries generally failed to keep up with cyclical trends and to supply such trends to the consumer, producing garments of poorer quality when they did.[12]

To announce the visit of Vice-President Nixon to the *American National Exhibition* held in Moscow in 1959, the cover of *Life* magazine was dedicated to 'World Leaders' Wives', showing Pat Nixon and Elena Khrushchev flanked by the wives of the Soviet senior ministers Anastas Mikoyan and Frol Kozlof (p.26). Pat Nixon, although never an American fashion icon in the mould of Jacqueline Kennedy, nevertheless cuts a smarter figure than her Eastern counterparts, particularly Mrs Kozlof, who is captured glancing askance at Mrs Nixon's dress.[13] At the exhibition, ready-to-wear fashion formed an important part of the image of an easy-going American lifestyle, as did the popular demonstrations by hairdressers and make-up artists (p.27).

Christian Dior, catwalk show. Moscow, 1959

The propagandizing potential of fashion was not ignored by the Soviets, despite the rhetoric of Soviet technological supremacy deployed at exhibitions. As a counterpart to the *American National Exhibition*, an exhibition of Soviet culture and achievement was sent to New York, where visitors could see displays of Sputniks, scientific instruments and models of power stations and nuclear ice-breaker ships. In June of that year, a show of Russian fashions was also staged in New York, and this event attracted a large crowd, causing one critic to report that 'it seemed clear proof that an atom smasher is a poor match for an attractive young lady in a well-fitted blouse'.[14] Back home in the same year, privileged Muscovites could enjoy the first couture collection shown by a Western designer in the Soviet Union, when the House of Dior was invited to stage its first catwalk show east of the Iron Curtain, as part of a French–Soviet policy of cooperation, as well as Khrushchev's initiative to 'learn from the West'.[15]

One of the central policies of the Khrushchev Thaw was the so-called Scientific-Technological Revolution, discussed first by Prime Minister Nikolai Bulganin in 1955, which then became the basis for an announcement to expand Soviet scientific research further, made by Khrushchev in 1961.[16] In the 1960s special attention was given to the research fields of plastics and electronics, and although, unlike the West, the Soviet regime did not often manage to translate research developments into material benefits for its people, it nevertheless did impact upon the use of synthetic fabrics in clothing and everyday goods. Within the Soviet sphere of influence, the development of specialist areas of research was seen not only as a way of 'building communism', but also a means by which member states could assert their influence in the bloc – the East German plastics programme was one such example of this, discussed below. To borrow a phrase from the American sociologist David Riesman, the competing East and West programmes of scientific and materials research constituted a kind of 'Nylon War'.

Viktor Koretsky, <u>From Oil We Take for the Needs of our Country a River of Gasoline, Oil and Petroleum and in Addition Thousands of Items for the Home and for Domestic Comfort!</u>. Poster. USSR, 1960

Sports Coat for Rainy Weather. Balloon silk,
designed for ÚBOK (Institute of Home and
Clothing Culture), Prague, 1969. Žena a móda
(April 1969)

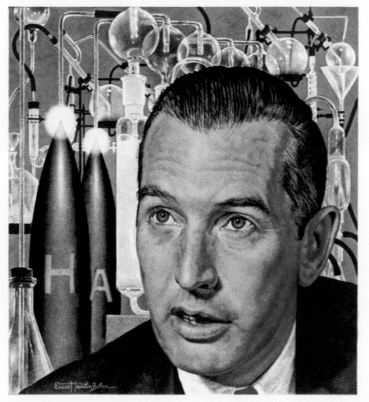

'Cellophane, nylon, a wrinkleproof suit — and the
H-bomb', cover of Time (16 April 1951), showing
Crawford Greenewalt, President of Dupont

SCIENCE

Listen to the sounds of the new words: cellulosic, polynosic, polyamide, polyester, acrylic, polypropylene, polyvinyl, spandex. These are new fibres from the laboratory. They are man-made, extruded through spinnerettes in liquid or molten streams. Their base is chiefly petro-chemical. They are controllable, uniform, predictable. They can be changed and designed for specific end uses. They are independent of natural phenomena.[17]

Since one of the chief arenas of East–West competition was science, material technologies counted among the prominent areas of Cold War research on both sides. Many new synthetics were part of the accelerated technological development of the period, often emerging from what has been called 'the military-industrial complex'.[18] The new fabrics of the 1950s and '60s were sometimes by-products of chemical research undertaken for military, aeronautical and space purposes. The petrochemical industries, boosted by massive government investment in both East and the West, were able to maintain unprecedented levels of research from the end of the Second World War to the early 1970s, when the industry was thrown into disarray by the oil crisis. In the USA, consumer capitalism and Cold War science often went hand in hand. Dupont, who had pioneered the development of nylon from the 1930s onwards, was also engaged in research into plutonium for the Manhattan Project, the war-time code name for the programme that developed the world's first nuclear weapons.[19] As the cover of *Time* magazine in 1951 attested, Dupont's products under development included 'cellophane, nylon, a wrinkleproof suit – and the H-bomb'.

Synthetics also became synonymous with affordable clothing, often in ways that played on their associations with modernity and youth. The qualities of the new plastics were embraced by designers seeking to exploit their different aesthetic and structural possibilities. Manufacturers looking for cost-effective alternatives to cotton and wool made use of synthetic fibres for an ever widening range of everyday goods and clothes. The functional qualities of synthetic fabrics were trumpeted by manufacturers; the new materials were crease-resistant, machine-washable and quick drying – although issues of flammability and the effects of wear and tear were usually avoided. In the 1950s the science of new 'wonder materials' had become the stuff of fiction: for example, in the Ealing Comedy *The Man in the White Suit* (directed by Alexander Mackendrik, 1951), a chemist invents a radioactive fabric that will never get dirty or wear out, throwing the textile industry into turmoil. Although his invention eventually proves fallible, the idea that science could offer such innovations was widely held.

Nylon, a highly flexible and wholly synthetic material, was the ultimate post-war plastic. A popular replacement for silk hosiery following its discovery at Dupont in the early 1930s, it was requisitioned for military use during the Second World War, causing a panic about stockings shortages. After the war, it emerged as a material so adaptable that its metaphorical associations alone can tell a history of post-war society. David Reisman's essay of 1951, 'The Nylon Wars', is a Cold War parody in which the USA launches a bombing mission over the Soviet Union – showering its communist 'enemies' with the plastic products of a modern 'democratic' society, in a concerted propaganda campaign of material abundance.[20]

Plastics were also to become part of everyday life in the socialist East. In the German Democratic Republic (DDR), for example, the 'Chemistry Programme' (Chemieprogramm) announced in 1958 was to be one of the chief drivers of the promised 'Scientific-Technological Revolution'.[21] Synthetic fibres, such as Dederon (the DDR name for nylon, chosen as an extension of the acronym for the socialist republic), were used to produce inexpensive clothing, as well as household goods. PVC, as in the West, was used for rainwear and boots, sometimes with a touch of high fashion to it. As Eli Rubin has described, 'From fashion shows to clothing racks in stores and closets everywhere, synthetic fibers such as Dederon and Malimo also almost completely replaced natural fibers, especially for women's clothing.'[22] Inexpensive non-iron and drip-dry synthetic fabrics (patented and marketed as brand names in the West such as Terylene and Crimplene) dominated mass fashion in the socialist republics throughout the 1960s, and were popular due to their fashionable colours and patterns, as Eva Hlaváčková has explored in the context of Czechoslovakia.[23] Although the command economies of the Eastern bloc lagged behind the West in their ability to turn their scientific innovations into material benefits for their citizens, they nevertheless employed the same rhetoric of a future, technological utopia. Plastics, heralded as the basis for modern life, were championed in East Germany under slogans such as 'Chemistry gives beauty, affluence and bread',[24] a similar sentiment to the phrase Dupont had employed since 1935, 'Better Things for Better Living, through Chemistry'. Becoming a by-line for the 1960s, Dupont's slogan had a massive effect on popular consciousness: amongst other uses, the adulterated phrase 'Better Living through Chemistry' was adopted by pro-drugs campaigners in the West.

The new synthetics of the post-war world had none of the solidity and inertness of the phenolic plastics of the 1920s and '30s, such as Bakelite. The thermoplastics of the 1950s, variants of polyethylene and polystyrene, were colourful, lightweight and malleable, capable of being poured and stretched into flexible shapes. Polyurethane, a flexible, polyester-based resin that is highly elastic, was developed into stretch fabrics such as Lycra, patented in 1959. PVC (polyvinyl chloride), a thermoplastic that can be used in a variety of forms, became best known for its fabric applications – shower curtains, boots, raincoats and also fetish wear. Synthetic rubber, like vinyl, was adapted into fashion in the 1960s, although the use of natural rubber in rainwear had begun almost 150 years before.

One of the defining characteristics of the new synthetics was their expendability: new materials that could be simply used up and thrown away were seen as positive benefits to a modern and efficient society. As the plastics historian Jeffrey Meikle has observed, this attitude to plastics reflected 'an expansive culture of impermanence' in the period.[25] In America, the novelty of disposability had been easily assimilated into everyday life. Rapid obsolescence became a fundamental characteristic of product design in the US in the 1950s, with seasonal model changes in cars and kitchen appliances, supported by a highly efficient advertising system, devoted to the maximization of profits. Needless to say, this phenomenon attracted critics, such as the American writer Vance Packard, who attacked the agencies of such a wasteful society in a series of books, culminating in *The Waste Makers* of 1961.[26]

Tesil dresses with appliqué circles
of black plastic. ÚBOK (Institute
of Home and Clothing Culture), Prague,
1969. <u>Žena a móda</u> (April 1970)

Paco Rabanne, paper dresses made from Vilbond
and coloured adhesive tape. Late 1960s

above left:
Paper dress, Waste Basket Boutique. 1967.
V&A: T.31-1992

above right
Paper dress, Dispo (Meyersohn & Silverstein
Ltd). Printed paper. 1967. V&A: T.181-1986

The ephemerality and expendability of American consumer goods were also seized upon by some designers in the 1950s and '60s, looking for ways to invigorate modern living with a sense of newness. The speeded-up nature of contemporary experience, it was felt, demanded a form of architecture and product design that could be readily renewed at any given moment. Expendability was a central tenet of Pop Art, as the design critic Reyner Banham explained in 1963: 'the aesthetics of Pop depend on a massive initial impact and small sustaining power, and are therefore at their poppiest in products whose sole object is to be consumed'.[27] The British architectural group Archigram, advocates for an expendable architecture, imagined 'instant' cities that could be plugged together and reconfigured at will, with a combination of prefabricated elements, multi-media and communications technologies.[28]

In fashion in the later 1960s, the fascination with disposability resulted in a trend for throwaway paper clothes. As with many material developments, it too came from the military, as an article in the *Chicago Tribune* in 1959 had made clear:

> *Do your clothes need to be cleaned or washed? Are you tired of the old patterns or colors? In the future, if your answer to any of these questions is yes, you'll simply throw the old clothes away – and maybe kindle a camp fire with them.*

> *Much of tomorrow's wearing apparel may be made out of treated paper, intended for use a few times, then for discard. The Quartermaster Corps is already investigating the use of such processed paper for parachutes, disposable uniforms, pup tents, and other shelters. It wears well, and its insulating qualities make it usable in all kinds of weather.*[29]

Although initially conceived as a suitable material for medical, as well as military use, paper-like fabrics made an immediate marketing impact in the late 1960s. The paper dress, which first appeared on the high street in 1966, could be bought for just a fraction of the cost of its fabric equivalent, worn a few times and then discarded. The Scott Paper Company produced a $1 paper dress in 1966 as a promotional gimmick. The Mars Manufacturing Company in West Asheville, North Carolina, converted from a hosiery company to a paper garment business in 1967, produced popular collections under the label Waste Basket Boutique (p.37).[30] Paco Rabanne and Ossie Clark both produced collections of paper garments in 1967, and small companies such as Dispo in London (designers Diane Meyersohn and Joanne Silverstein) set up to supply fashionable boutiques with such products (p.37). Rabanne's plastic-coated garments (made from Vilbond) were constructed using heat-welded seams, with coloured adhesive tape as both fixing and decoration, so no sewing was necessary (p.36). Rabanne also produced disposable nightwear for the Hilton hotel chain: 'Pacojamas' sold for approximately 15 francs, or $2, a pair.[31]

The paper-like fabrics used to manufacture disposable garments were actually made from unwoven textile such as cellulose fibre, producing a fabric that was hard to rip but easy to cut (resulting in a trend for customizing paper clothes, too). Paper fashions were not restricted to the West. Their supposed practicality and affordability were exploited by manufacturers in Eastern Europe, looking for alternative uses for synthetic materials. In East Germany, for example, a fashion magazine began a campaign in 1968 to promote dresses made from Vliesset, a rayon and plastic fibre printed paper. Offering 100 dresses free for readers to test, the magazine described them as highly fashionable, affordable and expendable after only five wears.[32] In Czechoslovakia, dresses made from Papitex, an unwoven textile composed of viscose and tesil (Terylene), were first produced for home consumption in 1970, marketed as garments for summer wear, to be thrown away after single use; capable of light laundering and ironing, their life might extend to a few wears.[33]

The fashion for paper clothing, however, was not to last – by the early 1970s it had suffered a decline in popularity similar to that of other synthetics, tainted by the loss of faith in the technological vision of the 1960s. Disposable clothing was the subject of sharp attack from the social critic Alvin Toffler, who saw a 'throw-away mentality' as a persistent weakness in 1960s culture:

> *The recent introduction of paper and quasi-paper clothing carried the trend towards disposability a step further. Fashionable boutiques and working-class clothing stores have sprouted whole departments devoted to gaily colored and imaginatively designed paper apparel. Fashion magazines display breathtakingly sumptuous gowns, coats, pyjamas, even wedding dresses made of paper.*[34]

Dresses so cheap that it became expedient to throw them away rather than pay the dry-cleaning bills were indicative of a mentality with 'a set of radically altered values with respect to property', argued Toffler.[35] Rather than being a novel aspect of modern, practical living, Toffler saw such disposable goods as evidence of a decreasing relationship between people and things, and a replacement of the values of permanence with those of transience: further evidence of the destabilized and incoherent nature of modern life.

THE SPACE AGE BODY

THE SPACE AGE BODY

The acceleration of technological competition between East and West in the post-war years made the dawn of the Space Age a reality. In 1957 the Soviet satellite Sputnik was successfully launched into orbit, an act of such technological audacity that it fired fears as well as hopes for the future. An aluminium sphere with trailing antennae, weighing only 184 pounds, it sent a signal around the world for 22 days that could be picked up on amateur radios. To some, the Sputnik 'bleep' signalled the threat of a new kind of warfare, which would be waged in the heavens as well as on earth. To others, it meant the birth of a technological age that might bring forth new forms of communication, perhaps new means of transportation and even human settlements in space. Shocked by the early lead taken by the Soviets in the Space Race, the USA announced a programme of space research, the most audacious aspect of which was President J. F. Kennedy's announcement in 1961 of the programme to put a man on the moon by 1970 (achieved, in fact, a year early, when Neil Armstrong and Buzz Aldrin made it there in *Apollo 11*).[1]

Apart from its fearful connotations, space exploration inspired a wave of utopian thinking about the future that took popular form. By the mid-1960s the futurism of the Space Race had been turned into a definite and wearable fashion 'look'. The core components of Space Age clothing – utilitarian body stockings or jumpsuits to provide a clean silhouette, over which were worn geometrically cut tunics, coats and mini dresses, and accessorized with go-go boots, wide belts and helmet – or visor-like headgear – dominated the catwalks and style magazines for several years. The look was assertive, utopian and even had militaristic connotations: the Space Age collections of Pierre Cardin were shown by models en masse, as if they were the crew of an arriving spaceship, perhaps the 'avant-garde' of a youthful and futuristic army.

Pierre Cardin, ready-to-wear
Cosmocorps collection. 1967

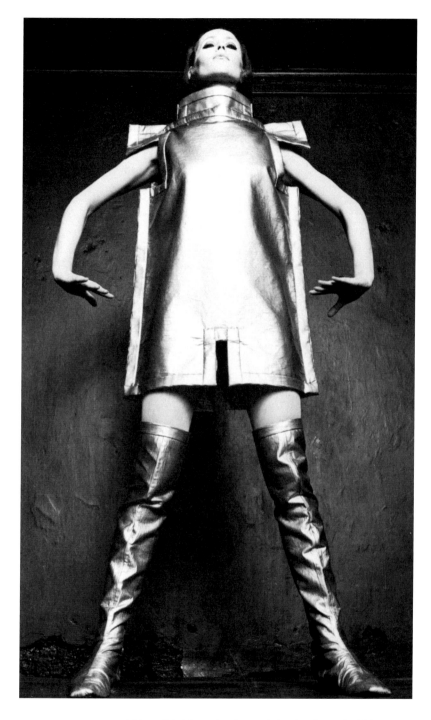

Alice Edeling, tunic and boots in metallic
fabric. The Netherlands, late 1960s

A JOURNEY INTO TOMORROW

Of course, futuristic fashion was not a preoccupation unique to the 1960s, although this was the first decade that it emerged as a characteristic of street wear. Clothing was an element of the novel, futuristic predictions made by designers throughout the twentieth century. For example, predictions for the year 2000, made at the time of the New York World's Fair in 1939 and published in American *Vogue*,[2] included Gilbert Rohde's 'Solosuit', an air-conditioned one-piece that could also receive and transmit electronic messages, worn by the man of the future:[3] 'His hat will be an antennae – snatching radio out of the ether. His socks disposable, his suit minus tie collar and buttons.'[4] The woman of the year 2000, on the other hand, would wear diaphanous, silvered and aluminium materials; have her body temperature controlled by an electronic belt, and her face illuminated by an electrical headdress.

Both electronics and synthetics were seen as prerequisites for future existence. At the *Daily Mail Ideal Home* exhibition in London in 1956, the architects Alison and Peter Smithson presented their 'House of the Future', a prefabricated home fashioned entirely from plastics, featuring all the components of imagined 'Space Age' living: artificial sunlight and climate control, electronic remote-controlled appliances, a self-cleaning bathroom.[5] The intended inhabitants were a young and childless professional couple, and the intended 'future' was 25 years hence, in 1981. The Smithsons imagined this future house as an industrial product, manufactured in a factory, made to be expendable and replaced with a sleeker model after a few years, just like a car. In fact, the House of the Future was consciously styled like an automobile. Although the house had a breezy and futuristic feel to it, it was also an appropriate, defensive environment for the nuclear age. As Beatrix Colomina has pointed out, its lack of exterior windows, its regulated environment and the suggestion of total isolation from the outside world marked out the House of the Future as a bunker.[6]

For the duration of the *Ideal Home* exhibition, the house was 'inhabited' by actors, playing out the scenarios of future domestic life. For this purpose, the sportswear designer (and former tennis player) Teddy Tinling was brought into the project to design an appropriate 'Space Age look' using synthetic fabrics, advised by James Laver, the costume historian and Victoria and Albert Museum curator.[7] Despite the Smithsons' conception of a labour-saving home where domestic tasks would not necessarily be assigned according to traditional gender roles, Tinling's costumes were a more conventional reflection of masculine/feminine roles. Out of doors, clothing for both men and women was to be plain and unembellished (the woman's dress 'almost as severe as the man's'), suggesting the need for clothes to suit a tough urban environment. At home, while the man might change into brightly coloured leisure wear (all made from a kind of nylon knitwear), the woman would wear 'light and pretty clothes': 'Through history women have emphasized their femininity by décolleté neckline', explained Tinling, 'and our women of the future will be no exception.'[8]

Alison and Peter Smithson, House of the
Future, living room. Clothing by Teddy
Tinling. Daily Mail Ideal Home Exhibition,
London. 1956

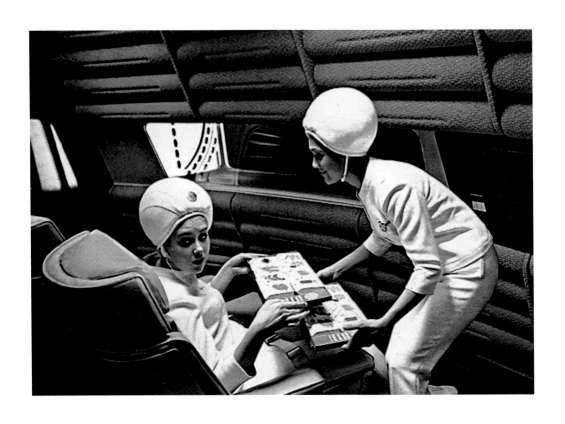

Hardy Amies, costumes for <u>2001: A Space Odyssey</u>,
directed by Stanley Kubrick. 1968

Emilio Pucci, 'Space Bubble' helmet
for Braniff airlines. Plastic. 1965

Gera Wernitz, costume designs for the
staff of the East Berlin Teletower.
Pen, watercolour and sample swatches. 1968

48

East Berlin Teletower. 1965-9

One crucial element of futuristic fashion was the idea of clothing as a uniform, as a means of stressing the practical and ordered nature of quasi-military dress. Uniforms also suggested glamorous and fantasy forms of travel, either by air or into space. In the early sequences of Stanley Kubrick's film *2001: A Space Odyssey* (1968), the flight to the space station is shown as a version of modern air travel, albeit in conditions of zero-gravity, with a female flight attendant dressed in Space Age tailoring designed by Hardy Amies (p.46). The brash and glamorous American airline Braniff had made the link between air and space travel in 1965, when they hired Emilio Pucci to redesign their flight attendant uniforms as part of a company makeover. The vibrantly coloured uniforms initially came accessorized with a 'Space Bubble' helmet to protect hairdos from being blown away when airside, but these were soon dropped as being impractical (p.47). The Space Age flight attendant look was also adopted in East Germany in 1968, for the East Berlin Teletower, a symbol of socialist technological superiority that was also promoted as a futuristic 'experience' for East Germans visiting the popular 'Telecafé' restaurant at the top of the revolving tower. The staff uniforms were designed as if for flight attendants, and featured 'a silver dederon-coated trench coat', and a 'narrow suit made of silver imitation leather, zippers on the pockets and at the centre of the frontpiece. Finely knitted shirt-jumper with lurex effect. Belt buckle made of plexiglass'.[9] Greeted by the sight of these attendants, visitors to the tower would be in no doubt that they were embarking on a journey into tomorrow.

FASHION FUTUROLOGISTS

In his critical account of the Swinging Sixties, *The Neophiliacs* (1969), Christopher Booker paid particular attention to the sight of young women in London wearing new, provocative and futuristic fashions. If a visitor from 1955 had suddenly been transported to London a decade later, Booker surmised, he would have been shocked by girls with their

> startling Op Art black and white, their shiny plastics, their little white Courrèges boots, above all, their hemlines which, during the summer, had risen two or three inches above the knee. Nothing would have surprised him more than the exhibitionistic violence with which these fashions grabbed at the attention – the contrasts, the jangling colours, the hard glossiness of PVC, the show of thigh.[10]

This was the look launched on the catwalks of Paris and in the boutiques of Swinging London, led by the pioneering designer Mary Quant. In Paris, a series of collections by Pierre Cardin, André Courrèges and Paco Rabanne in 1964–5 featured unconventional synthetic materials, a crisp modern palette of bright colours offset with white, black and silver, and a lean and angular silhouette for both men and women, achieved by using moulded and stiff fabrics that held their own shape rather than draped to the body. These clothes stressed a new kind of functionality: fastenings were made using zippers and Velcro; fabrics were riveted and welded as well as stitched. Given their interest in modern materials, constructional techniques and sculptural forms, the practice of these designers was frequently aligned with the tenets of modernist architecture; in fact, all three had had some form of architectural or engineering training.

The futuristic collections of the mid-1960s reflected a mood of technological optimism in France, as in Britain. In that decade, France was a nation undergoing a programme of technological modernization initiated by President de Gaulle. In 1960 he announced that France would be joining the Space Race, resulting in the foundation of the Centre Nationale d'Etudes Spatiales (CNES, the French equivalent of the American NASA) in 1961. The following year, he also announced that France would develop its own 'tactical nuclear deterrent' with a programme of long-range ballistic missiles and nuclear submarines. This assertive attitude towards technology contrasted sharply with French *travails* over decolonization, and the country's changing and uncertain international status in these years. Despite these anxieties, the economic modernization of France in the 1950s and '60s led to a more visible and assertive youth culture, with greater disposable income and consuming habits that were different from the previous generation – partly in response to the post-war impact of American popular culture. Of course, French youth culture also had its own basis in pop music and street culture, distinct from anglo-american trends. However, it was futuristic fashion which served as the main representation of French youthfulness abroad.[11]

The Space Age Body

Pierre Cardin, male and female models
in their versions of the Cosmos Ensemble.
Cream and red jersey respectively, both
with black vinyl over ribbed sweaters. 1966

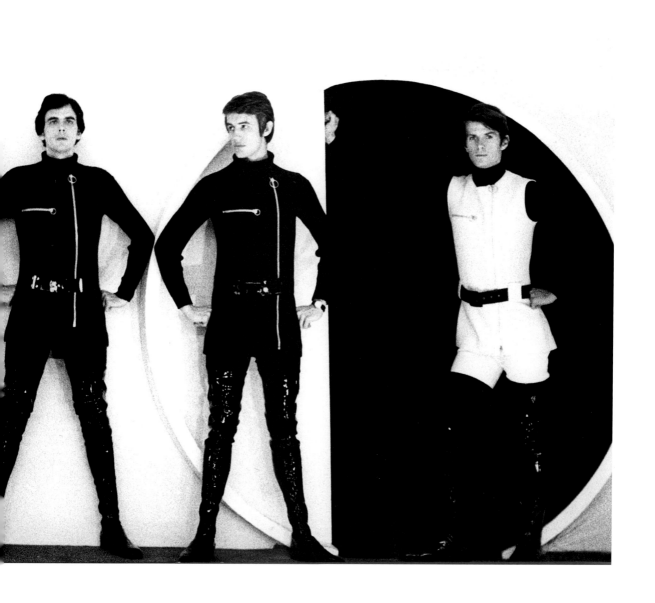

Pierre Cardin, ready-to-wear men's
collection. 1969. Photograph by Y.Takata

ANDRÉ COURRÈGES

The clothes of André Courrèges (produced under his name and co-designed with his wife, Coqueline) epitomize the ways in which Parisian fashion served as a channel for the optimism and technological modernity of the 1960s.[12] The designer, Courrèges argued, 'applies the maximum of his taste to the maximum in technological and social advances of his time'.[13] Trained as a civil engineer, Courrèges turned to fashion after the war, during which he had seen active service as a pilot. From 1950 to 1960 he worked with Balenciaga, before establishing a fashion house under his own name in 1961. Soon after he showed his first miniskirts and dresses, a development matched by Mary Quant in London.[14]

His ground-breaking collections of 1964–5 established him as the author of the 'Space Age' look: geometrically cut mini-dresses, tunics and trouser suits, made of double or triple gabardine so that they held their own structure, were shown with tops and shorts in Saint-Gall lace and worn with white boots (p.55). His collections used a palette of bright acid colours with large amounts of white and also silver. His emphasis on structure and clean, modernist forms stemmed from a long interest in architecture, particularly the work of Le Corbusier and Eero Saarinen, and he maintained that 'designing a building and making a dress have much in common'.[15] The precision and simplicity of his clothes are the results of the application of a kind of mathematical method to design, using basic geometrical forms in ways indebted to the principles of the Bauhaus school of design and the Russian Constructivists. After 1965 the Courrèges look was widely copied, resulting in his refusal to show publicly in 1966. In 1967, however, he produced a diffusion range of his 'Couture Future' collection. His menswear collections of 1968–9 featured triple-layered capes with balaclava hoods, worn with body stockings. Like his trademark eyewear, the hoods of these capes restrict the vision to a strip – a threatening look suggesting the need for protection from the blinding brightness of, perhaps, an atomic flash or burning star (p.56).

The Space Age Body

Courrèges, Spring Collection.
Paris, 1965. <u>Elle</u> (4 March 1965).
Photographed by Peter Knapp

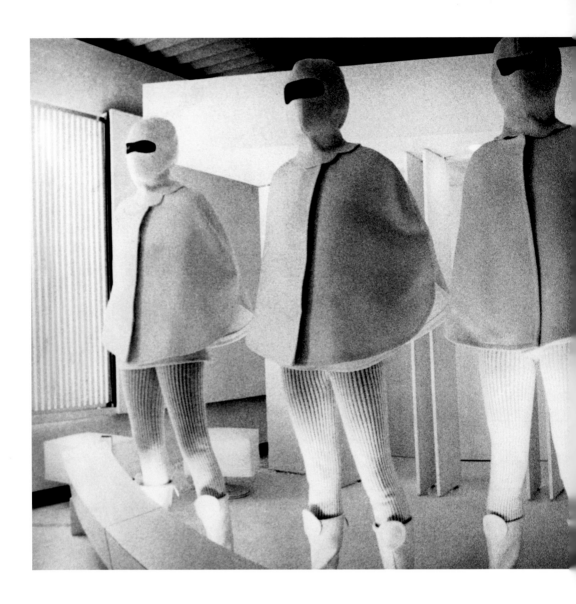

Courrèges, male models dressed in boots and
capes resembling cosmonauts. Autumn-Winter
collection 1968-9. Photographed by Peter Knapp

PIERRE CARDIN

The clothes I prefer are those for a life that doesn't exist yet – the world of tomorrow.[16]

The Italian-born Cardin moved to Paris in 1945, where he briefly studied architecture before working at the fashion houses of Paquin, Schiaparelli and then Dior in 1947. Setting up his own house in 1950, with a first couture collection in 1953, Cardin then broke with the traditions of the French couture system by producing a ready-to-wear collection in 1959. His collections showed a strong preference for angular shapes over body-hugging garments, achieved by using both highly structured and elastic materials. For this purpose, Cardin developed and patented 'Cardine', a material made from a synthetic wool substitute called Dynel (manufactured by Union Carbide), which could be vacuum-formed and bonded instead of cut and sewn into garments.[17] The moulding process enabled Cardin to produce three-dimensional reliefs on fabrics, so that the clothes have a sculptural quality to them. He also used geometric and futuristic motifs – such as circles and triangles, lightning bolts and targets – either as cut-outs or appliquéd onto vinyl. These motifs suggested the insignia of some kind of troop or team. More than any other designer in the period, Cardin's clothes propose the Space Age look as literally a uniform for youth, as shown in his Cosmos collections of 1967 (pp.51–53).

The Space Age Body

above:
Pierre Cardin, ready-to-wear, 1969

left:
Pierre Cardin, ready-to-wear. 1968

PACO RABANNE

My clothes are like weapons. When they are fastened they make
a sound like the trigger of a revolver.[18]

Rabanne's career developed rather differently from that of Cardin and Courrèges.
He arrived in Paris to study architecture at the Ecole des Beaux-Arts in 1951,
earning an income by designing accessories for various suppliers to the main Paris
fashion houses. His designs for handbags, buttons and jewellery made considerable
use of plastics (particularly Rhodoid), and he acquired the techniques not only for
stitching, but also for moulding, glueing and riveting materials together. Courrèges,
Cardin, Balenciaga and Givenchy were among the fashion houses to make use of his
accessories, and by 1965 he had established his name as a maker of plastic jewellery.

Rabanne's fascination with synthetics paralleled that of several architectural
groups working in Paris at the time, particularly the Utopie Group, known to Rabanne
through his friendship with the architect Antoine Stinco.[19] In the late 1960s Utopie
devised various forms of inflatable structures, exploring ideas of lightness, mobility
and obsolescence. The plastic inflatable building, according to Stinco, was a 'joyous
critique of gravity [and] of boredom with the world'.[20] Another colleague of Rabanne
was Quasar Khan, a French-Vietnamese designer of inflatable furniture, whose
wife, Emmanuelle Khahn, was a fashion designer who regularly employed Rabanne's
accessories. Quasar and Emmanuelle Khahn even produced dresses made from
transparent plastic. Together, these friends formed a small network of material
experimentalists in Paris, crossing boundaries between fashion, architecture and
interior design.

Rabanne's favoured material, Rhodoid, was light and flexible enough to be used
for clothing as well as jewellery. Cut from sheets into strips or discs, the plastic could
be punched and joined together with metal rings, producing a layered effect, either
for overlapping hanging garments or curved to make visors or helmets. Soon, the
effect produced with Rhodoid discs was extended to garments, which garnered press
attention and began selling through the Paris boutique Dorothée. Rabanne's first
official collection under his own name was shown in February 1966 – announced as a
collection of 'Twelve Unwearable Dresses in Contemporary Materials', worn by barefoot
models in the Hotel George V in Paris. He was never a couturier in the conventional
sense, and his skills were those of the artisanal craftsman or the experimental engineer.
'He's not a couturier', Coco Chanel was to comment, 'he's a metal worker'.[21] In 1966
Rabanne adapted a ready-made aluminium fabric called Lamex for fashion use. The
material, consisting of tiny metal discs linked with rings, was produced to make heavy
protective aprons for butchers (similar in its defensive capacity to chain mail). Using
a similar system of metal plates, discs and rings, Rabanne created other custom-made
metal fabrics, such as the Aluminium dresses of 1968, where the metal has been
hammered or studded to produce different decorative effects (pp.62–63).

Rabanne also developed a method of making single-piece plastic rainwear
(called 'Giffo'), using a process of spraying a cloud of plastic into a mould, which,

Paco Rabanne, plastic dress in white
and orange, From _Vogue_ UK, April 15,
1966. Photograph by David Montgomery

Dresses by Paco Rabanne, shown at The 37th
Home Furnishings Fair. 'Everything is Made
of Steel, from the Pots to the Chefs',
(4 March 1968)

opposite left:
Paco Rabanne, disc mini-dress (detail).
Perspex paillettes and metal chain. c.1967.
V&A: T.165-1983

opposite right:
Paco Rabanne, leather and metal dress
(detail). 1968. V&A: T.99-1988

when dry, could be peeled away and worn immediately. Although the Giffo rainwear never went into full-scale production, prototypes of it were shown in 1968 (p.64). Rabanne's enthusiasm for industrial materials and processes encompassed his use of thin rubber tubing to create fringed dresses (1966) and various forms of plastic-coated paper. The unconventional nature of the material alone was not his primary interest, but rather the opportunities these materials gave to use alternatives to stitching – such as welding or heat-sealing edges. Using an edging technique adapted from the machine production of architects' plans, Rabanne devised a method of paper dress production that could make one dress every three minutes.[22] He also applied his patented method of assembly to other fabrics, such as fur, leather and vinyl, as in a mini-dress made from panels of leather linked by metal studs. These more earthy garments captured a different 1960s aesthetic – not the shiny, silvered, Space Age look, but the primitive or Iron Age warrior woman. Both aesthetics were memorably combined in Roger Vadim's *Barbarella* (1968), for which Rabanne designed the costumes (p.65).

Rabanne's 'unwearable' dresses were in reality truly uncomfortable, the chain mail heavy, the metal cold, the edges of the plastic sharp and chafing. Nevertheless, they were designed for movement, with enough articulation in the material surface to enable it to follow the curves of a body, or give way to the movement of limbs. They attracted equal amounts of ridicule and wonder in the press. Despite using a cheap and readily available plastic, the early dresses were expensive, given the large amount of labour each took to produce. Their purpose, therefore, as Rabanne made clear, was as 'manifestos' – statements of purpose that would question the basis of clothing production and the wearer's attitude to fashion: 'Who knows what clothes will be? Maybe an aerosol used to spray the body, maybe women will be dressed in coloured gases adherent to their body, or in halos of light, changing colour with the movements of the sun or with their emotions.'[23]

 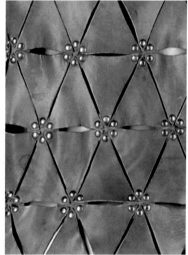

left:
Paco Rabanne, yellow moulded Giffo
rainwear. 1968

above:
Film still, Barbarella, directed by
Roger Vadim. 1968

HIGH KICKS, CATSUITS AND BODY ARMOUR

The armoured and uniformed Space Age look was popularized, and even made kitsch, by television shows such as *Star Trek* (from 1966) and *The Avengers* (1961–9). The stretch nylon jumpsuits, PVC boots and uniform insignias worn in popular TV series demonstrated how quickly the characteristics of Space Age fashion were taken up by costume designers, and how easily replicable the look was. The basis of the futuristic look that took hold in the popular imagination was the body stocking or jumpsuit, derived from sportswear, in particular skiwear or dance costume, with allusion to hi-tech undergarments designed for space and flight wear.

The jumpsuit was unisex, ideally made from synthetic materials (to allow for the elasticity of fit needed), and thought to be highly utilitarian. On the other hand, it was very revealing, produced an exaggerated silhouette and permitted great freedom of movement, therefore lending itself to the impression of an assertive female sexuality with an exaggerated physicality. It never worked quite the same way for men, as Ruben Torres' attempt to popularize the jumpsuit as menswear in 1967 shows (see p.13). In the long-running ABC television series *The Avengers*, the character of Emma Peel, played by Diana Rigg and introduced to the series in autumn 1965, exemplified this image. Designed by John Bates, Emma Peel's wardrobe featured figure-hugging catsuits, zippers, boots, stretch jersey and leather-look PVC. Apart from the arch and sometimes surreal humour of the series, *The Avengers* was characterized by

above:
Rudi Gernreich, unisex collection, 1970.
Photograph by Patricia Faure, 1973

left:
Ascher, après ski jacket. Mohair. 1960.
V&A: T.260-1988

Catsuit designed for Diana Rigg, in the
television series The Avengers. 1969

Rudi Gernreich, black wool-knit maillot
with black patent leather belt, black
vinyl hip boots and purple sun visor.
Photograph by William Claxton. 1965

the role reversal of the fighting sequences. Peel's side-kick, Steed (played by Patrick Macnee), elegantly suited and rather dandified, usually accessorized with bowler hat and furled umbrella, occupied the more staid role, whereas Emma Peel's action scenes consisted of high kicks and karate moves. Bates's successful look was also turned into a high-street fashion collection, produced under his label 'Jean Varon' as 'The Avengers Collection'. Although Diana Rigg's look on the show ranged from Jackie Kennedy-style skirt suits (such as a lavender crêpe dress and jacket, designed by Alun Hughes for Thomas of Mayfair in 1967, also available on the high street) to 'humorous' allusions to the show's Britishness (using tweed and tartan, for example), the catsuit and Emma Peel have remained synonymous.

The body stocking also suited the highly structured yet revealing clothing of designers like Courrèges, who put body stockings under tunics, or under garments featuring cut-outs. The use of highly elastic textiles in the form of knitted tubes suggested immense freedom of movement, and this was often emphasized by dance-like catwalk performances. Both Emilio Pucci and Rudi Gernreich had been instrumental in developing body-conscious clothing that did away with underlying structures, lining and seams, emphasizing a skinny, flat-chested and angular body shape. In fact, Gernreich became notorious for his proposal of 1964 for the 'topless bathing suit', modelled by his long-term collaborator and muse, Peggy Moffitt. Suggested as a social provocation rather than a commercial proposition in the first instance, Gernreich intended the suit to be a statement of freedom rather than titillation (3,000 garments were eventually produced, resulting in only two recorded appearances, one ending in arrest).[24]

Gijs Bakker and Emmy van Leersum, Dutch avant-garde jewellers who pushed their practice towards designing more extreme forms of body wear in the 1960s, produced a series of bodysuits for two exhibition-cum-performances in 1967 and again in 1970, the second entitled *Clothing Suggestions*.[25] The body stockings, made from highly elastic textile, were worn by dancers and friends, as well as the designers themselves, during performances featuring music and strobe lights. The garments were used to display jewellery designed by Bakker and Van Leersum, but were also worn unadorned, suggesting that body, clothing and jewellery had fused into a single silhouette. Instead of jewellery, these unadorned suits featured cut-outs in the material, with underlying structures that altered the natural body shape and drew attention to breasts and genitalia. Plastic tubes and forms were inserted into the fabric to distort the form of the body, defining or accentuating certain body parts, such as knee, elbow and hip joints.

Yet, inasmuch as 1960s fashion was concerned with revealing flesh, it also demonstrated a concern for armouring the body. Figure-hugging catsuits were often shown with chain mail, rigid plastic or metal breastplates and protective coverings for limbs. These body coverings are a kind of hybrid of clothing and jewellery design, and beg the question: what did the vulnerable body need protection from? In William Klein's film of 1966, *Qui êtes-vous, Polly Maggoo?*, a fashion show takes place in which the designer dresses the models entirely in aluminium sheets, for which he is rewarded with the approval of the critics, who dub him 'the poet of sheet-metal!'[26] As with Rabanne's Unwearable Dresses, the contrast between bare skin and cold metal was disquieting as well as seductive.

Gijs Bakker, Emmy van Leersum
and Tiny Leeuwenkamp, <u>Clothing</u>
<u>Suggestions</u>. Artificial
material, white tricot. 1970

Gijs Bakker and Emmy van Leersum played with the juxtaposition of soft skin and hard metal in their mid-1960s experiments with alternative body wear. Pushing jewellery to the extreme, they created giant collars, armbands and head pieces using industrial materials such as aluminium and plastic. Their philosophy, outlined in a statement of 1967, was to challenge the conventions of jewellery by engaging with the practices of both industrial design and modern art. What they wished to produce was 'a fusing of human body, of metal forms and of clothes design into a single aesthetic unity'.[27] After an exhibition in London in 1967, the press heralded the couple's work as the 'look of the year 2000'. In fact, Bakker and Van Leersum conceived of their work as something beyond fashion, towards sculpture, with the intention of exploring the relationship between the body and its environment.

Gijs Bakker, neck ornament: shoulder piece. Aluminium. 1967

Gijs Bakker, stovepipe necklace and bracelet. Purple anodized aluminium. 1967

The Space Age Body

Models dressed in metal sheets, from
the film <u>Qui êtes-vous, Polly Maggoo?</u>,
directed by William Klein. 1966

THE SPACESUIT

> *... when Homo Americanus finally sets foot on the moon it will be just as*
> *well the gravity is only one sixth of earth's for he is likely to be so hung*
> *about with packages, kits, black boxes and waldos that he would have*
> *a job to stand under any heavier 'g'.*[28]

No single garment encapsulated the changed relationship between technology and the body in the Cold War better than the spacesuit. Developing from experiments with high-altitude flight suits designed for pilots during the Second World War, by the 1960s the spacesuit had evolved into a technologized micro-habitat that replicated the conditions necessary for human survival: temperature, pressure, oxygen supply, waste removal and communication devices were brought together in an unparalleled fusion of technology with clothing, as Bradley Quinn has described it.[29] Spacesuits provided inspiration in the 1960s to designers of clothing, buildings or interiors (sometimes combining all three), who were fascinated by the possibilities of such human transcendence. The idea of the spacesuit as life-sustaining also lent itself to projections of future conditions on earth: not only could the dangers of modern life be countered by high-performance clothing, but also sensory experiences might be amplified by the use of wearable technologies.

Of course, it would be simplistic to characterize the protective suits of cosmonauts and astronauts as nearly clothing – rather they were complex syntheses of life-support and communications apparatus housing the body, as Reyner Banham suggests in his satirical description of astronautical kit above. The spacesuit operates as a prosthetic extension of the human body, where the relationship between user and tool is merged, and technology 'incorporated' to the extent that the body itself is reconfigured.[30] This envisaging of a new kind of human subject had an ideological motivation, under military conditions – as Deane Simpson has observed, the first Soviet cosmonauts were conceived as the ideal embodiment of the 'New Soviet Person'.[31]

The first spacesuits were on the whole adaptations of aeronautical pressure suits, developed for pilots from the 1930s onwards. Usually made from Neoprene rubber-coated fabrics, they were designed to combat the effects of high altitudes and rapid acceleration. For the first manned space mission of 1961, the high-pressure SK1 flight suit designed for Yuri Gagarin by the Soviet design bureau Zvezda was made from orange nylon with a built-in visored helmet and an inflatable collar for use in the event of a water landing. The pressure lining suit carried hose connections for life support and communications. Boots and gloves were made from heavy leather. The suits designed for NASA's Project Mercury (1958–63), which would result in the first American manned space flights, used a similar suit developed from a high-altitude pressure suit, with a silver layer of Mylar added to the Neoprene rubber coating. The suits were worn unpressurized and therefore soft, since the pressurized suit was necessary only in the event of an emergency.

The design of spacesuits was to alter substantially in preparation for the first space walk and eventually moon landing. For this, the suit had to be entirely

Research prototype for ORLAN
E.V.A. (extra-vehicular activity)
spacesuit. USSR, 1960s

self-supporting. The first space walk, by the cosmonaut Alexei Leonov in 1964, was made in a Zvezda-designed Berkut EVA (extra-vehicular activity) suit, which had to carry a portable life-support system. The EVA suit designed by NASA for the Apollo mission (1968–75) moon landings incorporated the following components: a first layer of water-cooled underwear (a network of thin tubing that circulated cool water); a triple-layered pressure suit, manufactured largely from nylon with a Neoprene coating; five further layers of aluminium-coated Mylar, each interlaid with a layer of Dacron for heat protection; two layers of Kapton for further heat protection; and two outer layers of Teflon-coated cloth. Helmet, boots and gloves were made from high-strength materials such as polycarbonate, with pressure seals and silicone rubber components to permit a degree of movement and tactile sensing. The helmet was changed from a close-fitting design to one that permitted the wearer to move his head freely inside. When inside the spacecraft, the suit would be connected to the internal life-support systems; on leaving, the wearer would don a backpack capable of sustaining life for seven hours, for controlling body temperature, maintaining pressure, air and waste removal.

Despite the heaviness and restricted movement experienced by astronauts, the spacesuit inspired a generation of experimental designers and architects, for whom it represented a kind of liberation from the merely physical or corporeal. The Austrian architect Hans Hollein, for example, described the spacesuit (along with the jet helmet and the space capsule) as the ideal 'minimum' dwelling.[32] The spacesuit was seen as the embodiment of a controlled environment containing within it the elements needed for life support, including oxygen, temperature control and waste removal. Electronic systems were incorporated to provide communications contact, as well as to monitor the condition of the body. In order to stay alive, the astronaut's body was regulated homeostatically – the maintenance of a stable condition, based on constant monitoring or feedback. In his complete dependence upon non-organic means to keep him alive, the astronaut's body was effectively merged with technology; he became a kind of cyborg. In an article of 1960, NASA scientists Manfred Clynes and Nathan Kline proposed that, rather than designing spacesuits that could support the human body in space by mechanical and electronic means, science should develop human–machine hybrids – or cyborgs (see p.81) – with the physical capacity to survive in space, thus freeing up their human capacity 'to explore, to create, to think, and to feel'.[33] In the next chapter, the idea of architecture, clothing and technology as the prosthetic extension of the human body – the cybernetic body – will be explored more fully.

This is ground control to Major Tom
You've really made the grade
And the papers want to know whose shirts you wear
Now its time to leave the capsule if you dare

David Bowie, Space Oddity, 1969

The Space Age Body

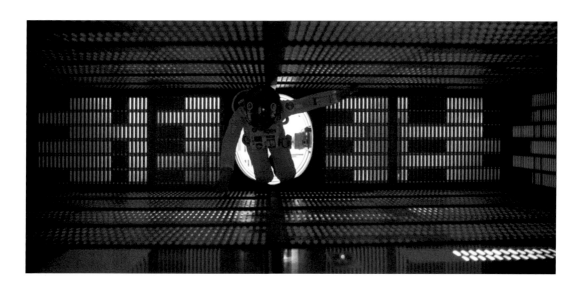

Astronaut Dave Bowman (played by Keir Dullea) inside
the computer HAL. Still from <u>2001: A Space Odyssey</u>,
directed by Stanley Kubrick. 1968

THE CYBERNETIC BODY

THE CYBERNETIC BODY

Cold War science offered the means by which the future body could be imagined as an enhanced technological version of the human self. The image of man invaded by technology or mutated by science has long been the basis of science-fiction fantasies, stemming from precursors such as Mary Shelley's novel *Frankenstein* (1818) and Fritz Lang's film *Metropolis* (1926-7).[1] By the 1960s the Space Race provided the image of body and technology brought into intimate contact, where the boundaries between human and mechanical function became increasingly difficult to discern. This melding of the body with technology became the subject of exploration for many designers, expressed in terms of both clothes and buildings.

One seductive idea of technology-enhanced sensory experience came from the psychedelic music and nightclub scene in the mid- to late 1960s. Nightclubs and art happenings used the 'mind-expanding' effects of multiple light projections merged with sound and movement, as at Andy Warhol's multi-media experience called *The Exploding Plastic Inevitable* (1966–7), which featured music by the Velvet Underground, projections of Warhol's films, performance and dance (p.78). In 1968 the dance choreographer Alwin Nikolais discussed how clothing might be designed to perform differently in these environments, by incorporating flashing lights or using the body as a screen. 'A new social thinking is indicated', he suggested, 'by the desire, particularly on the part of young people, to experience an environment by moving in the midst of beating sound and shifting lights, colours and shapes.'[2] The American designer Diana Dew had already begun to incorporate lighting into fashion in 1966, using a portable, rechargeable battery power pack to illuminate the electroluminescent films and pliable plastic lamps she used in her clothing. Sold through the modish boutique Paraphernalia in New York (which was also part of the New York Warhol scene), Dew described her clothing as 'hyperdelic transsensory experiences', adding that the limited lifespan of the garments could be enhanced by a more efficient power supply: 'If a girl wants to flash for ten hours, she'll have to get a bigger battery.'[3] Electroluminescent films were also incorporated into garments by the Austrian architecture group Haus-Rucker, who produced body suits in 1968 (p.82).

The sensory effects that could be achieved by electronic light and sound effects were the bases for many design experiments of the later 1960s. Architectural groups such as Archigram from Britain (Warren Chalk, Ron Herron, Dennis Crompton, Peter Cook, David Greene and Michael Webb), the Austrian collectives Coop Himmelblau (Wolf D. Prix, Helmut Swiczinsky and Michael Holzer) and Haus-Rucker Co (Laurids Ortner, Günter Zamp-Kelp and Klaus Pinter), and the French group Utopie (architects Jean Aubert, Jean-Paul Jungmann and Antoine Stinco, with sociologists including Jean Baudrillard) proposed prototypical structures that merged the concepts of architecture and clothing to create intimate habitats for the liberation of consciousness. The work of this experimental generation coalesced around the theme of technology (excited by its possibilities but also often expressing concern for its ecological and social implications). Rarely afforded the opportunity to build 'real' buildings, they explored these concerns on paper, through models and working prototypes, and in the context

Diana Dew, electroluminescent dress.
Photograph by Edward Pfizenmaier. 1966

of exhibitions and happenings. Many projects were conceived as provocations, but their work was not only fantastical, since it was largely based on the adaptation of technical and engineering possibilities derived from military and scientific exploration.[4] The environments they proposed were often ephemeral and portable, sometimes housed in inflatable structures, packed with electronics to supply air, light, music, rhythm and vibration. Like spacesuits and spacecraft, they cocooned the wearer/ occupier in an artificial, technologically supported capsule. This chapter explores these projects, with their roots in the technologies of the Cold War, as expressions of both the hopes and the fears of the 1960s.

The futuristic vision of the technology-enhanced human stemmed from the discipline of cybernetics: the study of the relationship between humans and inorganic systems. In 1960 scientists Manfred Clynes and Nathan Kline had coined the term cyborg (cybernetic organism) to describe a man 'enhanced' by technology who could survive in outer space. With electronics and artificial organs embedded in his body, the cyborg would look human, but would have bodily functions adapted for life in space – respiration would be artificial (no need for fully functioning lungs or airways) and speech would be transmitted from the vocal cords via radio. This, they argued, would be a more efficient form of research than developing spacesuits as life-support systems for the (un-enhanced) human body:

> *If man in space, in addition to flying his vehicle, must continuously be checking on things and making adjustments merely in order to keep himself alive, he becomes a slave to the machine. The purpose of the Cyborg... is to provide an organizational system in which such robot-like problems are taken care of automatically and unconsciously, leaving man free to explore, to create, to think, and to feel.*[5]

Clynes and Kline saw this vision of man's evolution as liberating, but for others this vision of technology was insidious – a metaphor for the invasion of human privacy by other agencies. In his apocalyptic novel of 1961, *The Soft Machine*, William S. Burroughs predicted how the future human body would be invaded by mechanical and media technologies: 'under siege from a vast hungry host of parasites with many names'.[6] Burroughs's fiction, set within the context of paranoia concerning late consumer capitalism and corporatism, technological acceleration and the geopolitics of the Cold War, mined a rich seam of dystopian fantasy, which has continued in film and fiction, to include William Gibson's novel of 1984, *Neuromancer*, and films such as *Blade Runner* (1982) and *The Matrix* (1999).

Haus-Rucker-Co, Electric Skin 1, 1968

The Cybernetic Body

Rudi Gernreich, plastic armour
designed for a Max Factor promotion.
Photograph by William Claxton

THE EXTENSIONS OF MAN

By the time of Burroughs's writing, cybernetics had become established as the primary science for the understanding of systems, both biological and technological, and the interaction of human and mechanical action. The discipline of cybernetics grew out of military research in the 1940s into the relationships between humans and machines. The American mathematician Norbert Wiener, analysing ways in which the operator of an anti-aircraft gun would anticipate the trajectory of a moving target, developed a framework for the study of human–machine symbiosis. Wiener argued that the constant supply of information to both people and computers caused the modification of behaviour over time (which he called 'feedback'). Without this modification, people or systems would be subject to entropy, or deterioration. By understanding and anticipating this self-regulation in response to information, systems and behaviours could be made more efficient.[7]

Cybernetics became influential in a remarkable number of arenas: the development of computing and weaponry, of systems theory and business organization, and the sociological and psychological study of human behaviour. It formed the basis for the development of artificial intelligence (which had stemmed from Alan Turing's prediction of sentient computers in 1950), and for imagining the development of human–machine hybrids, or cyborgs.

This vision of a man–machine fusion, built upon military behaviours, was a powerful analogy for the extension of human capabilities by technology. 'The mythology of the cockpit', as the Austrian critic Georg Schöllhammer put it in 1998, 'ran through the whole period of the fifties and sixties ... the fantasy of the all powerful pilot, seated in his machine, remote from the consequences of his actions.'[8] For designers, this was both a terrifying and an inspiring vision. It influenced proposals for how human operators would interact within a confined space, controlling workspace or computer terminals, as in Robert Probst's design for the 'All-Action Office' for the manufacturer of furniture and office equipment Herman Miller (1964). Probst's idea for a workstation based on the necessary movements and actions undertaken by operatives became a standard model for the development of office spaces in the US in the 1960s.[9] Whereas his design was based on a rationalization of human actions (a continuation of the time and motion studies of the 1920s[10]), other designers in the same decade explored the ways in which cybernetics could inform a more playful and experimental development of interaction, as we shall see below.

Norbert Wiener's first books on cybernetics were, surprisingly, bestsellers, because his accessible explanations fuelled the collective vision (both fearful and hopeful) of a machine-led future.[11] A genre of film of the 1950s and '60s explored the possibility of artificial intelligence, usually the scenario of the super-computer that develops a mind of its own, with terrifying consequences.[12] HAL, the murderous, chess-playing computer in Kubrick's *2001: A Space Odyssey*, is one such non-human villain. Cybernetics offered much to the observers of culture in the 1960s, eager to

Raymond Loewy, design for a stateroom with individual work
and sleep mode, undertaken for NASA. Postercolour, pen
and ink and chalk on brown card. 1968. V&A: E.3203-1980

understand how fast-paced technological change was affecting modern society. Chief
among these voices was Marshall McLuhan, a Canadian professor of literature, who,
armed with an understanding of Wiener's theories, produced the most influential
analysis of the effects of information overload on culture and behaviour. In *Understanding Media* (1964), McLuhan argued that a combination of new technologies
– chiefly television, satellite communication and computing – had thrown an immense
'cosmic membrane' around the world, pulling everyone together in a 'global village'
in which time and distance were increasingly irrelevant.[13]

For McLuhan, following a cybernetic model, these new forms of media also
constituted an 'extension of man'. Just as new industrial products had once provided
a prosthetic extension of mechanical human operations, electronic products would
form a relationship to the human nervous system, modifying human behaviour through
their interaction (in cybernetic terms, a process of feedback). Television, as McLuhan
put it, was the most significant of the electronic media because it permeated nearly
every home in the country, 'extending the central nervous system of every viewer'.[14]
This evocative vision caught the imagination of a generation of designers and architects,
keen to imagine what new forms both technologies and bodies would assume in the
future. McLuhan's writings influenced many designers in their explorations of the
sensory and psychological possibilities of technology. His conviction that technological
change would bring about social change, challenging political hegemony with alternative
social, tribal allegiances, appealed to a 1960s generation tired of the sterile atmosphere
of Cold War politics.

CLOTHING AS COMMUNICATION

In art and design, cybernetics became influential partly because of the emphasis it placed on communication: the continual 'feedback loop' of information that circulated around people and systems. The idea that people, technologies and art could be responsive to environmental and social change, developing a more interactive form of behaviour, encouraged artists to engage with the idea of 'self-organization'. In 1965 the British conceptual artist Stephen Willats designed clothing based on kits that could be organized by the wearer to make multiple clothing types, such as 'Variable Sheets' (1965), which he called clothing for 'a new kind of reality' and part of a 'cybernetic vision of the future'.[15] Panels of coloured PVC zipped together to form coats and dresses and geometric symbols made from Perspex could be attached in different configurations to the panels; words could be inserted into the clear plastic panels to send messages to or from the wearer, who also wore visored helmets. For Willats, such garments were essays in communication, and explored the idea of art (and fashion) as a means of social exchange. The pieces were, in his words, 'amplification of the notion of self-organisation', a concept Willats had developed from his knowledge of contemporary organization theory, which he was familiar with through the work of the British cybernetician William Ross Ashby.[16] Willats also extended his use of cybernetic theory to the study of social interaction in urban spaces, for example, in his collaboration with the inhabitants of low-income housing, in order to understand the ways in which urban planning worked as a form of social control, and how this could be counteracted by individual behaviours. He continued for the next two decades to explore the communicative functions of clothing, in projects that extended this original conception.

Stephen Willats, PVC dress:
Variable Sheets (detail). PVC
and metal zippers. 1966. V&A:
T.19-1991

The Cybernetic Body

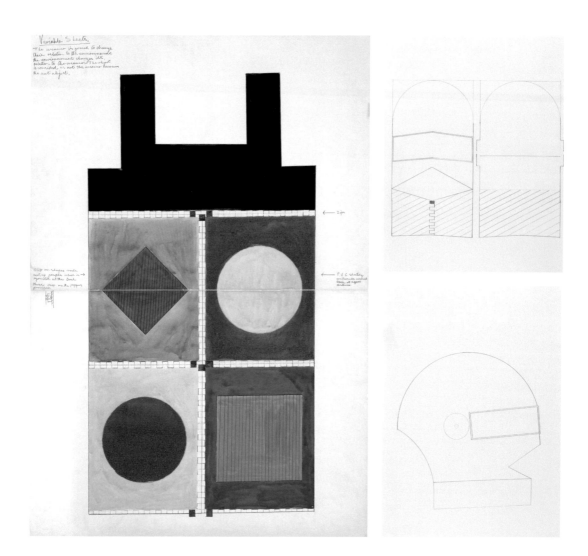

left:
Stephen Willats, design drawing for PVC
dress: <u>Variable Sheets</u>. Pencil and bodycolour
on paper. 1965. V&A: E.1615-1984

right:
Stephen Willats, design drawings for helmet.
V&A: E.1616 to 1618-1984

Václav Cigler, <u>Face Ornament</u>. 1968-9

In Czechoslovakia in the late 1960s the artist Václav Cigler also became fascinated
with the ways in which body adornment could act as a form of communication or
social observation. He designed a series of jewellery pieces composed of shiny metal
discs, held on the body by thick metal wires, which could either hang around the
neck, twist around the arm or be worn on the brow. The discs acted like mirrors –
when angled, they gave the wearer a view of the room they were in or of the people
around them, allowing the possibility of intimate eye contact or perhaps covert
observation. Cigler, also well known for his highly conceptual work in glass sculpture
and land art, viewed jewellery as 'landscape for the human body', as a means of
connecting the body with its environment.[17] His work as a teacher at the Bratislava
school of design (Vysokéj škole výtvarných umění v Bratislavě) from 1965 to 1979
inspired a generation of students to think about design in ways that were conceptual
and provocative, even though the turn of Czechoslovak politics after the Prague
Spring of 1968 imposed restrictions on the ways in which artists could work.[18]

Václav Cigler, <u>Circle Framing a Face</u>. 1968

WEARABLE TECHNOLOGIES

Spring of 1968 imposed restrictions on the ways in which artists could work.[18]

McLuhan's idea of the technological extensions of man fuelled what Schöllhammer has called 'the Cyborg fantasy of an apparatus for liberating consciousness from its organic and physiological basis within the human body'.[19] Cybernetic systems were imagined as taking the form of wearable technologies that could create personal and immersive media environments, precursors of the virtual reality experiments of the 1990s.[20] Predictions of such environments in the period often imagined television as the basis for virtual worlds. In 1960 the *Chicago Tribune* discussed the predictions of Hugo Gernsback, an electronics entrepreneur who was best known as the founder of the science-fiction magazine *Amazing Stories* (begun in 1926), which specialized in futuristic imaginings:

> Today's television receivers may one day be replaced by devices that will
> 'tickle' the brain, breaking right through to man's inner consciousness.
> At least that's what electronics trailblazer Hugo Gernsback believes.
> Brain tissue conducts electricity. What would be more logical then, asks
> Gernsback, than the development of a 'superceptor' whose impulses
> would create images directly in the mind, like dreams, instead of lighting
> up a television screen?[21]

The American computer scientist Ivan Sutherland had developed the first head-mounted virtual reality headsets in 1968, dubbed 'the incredible helmet', although these contraptions were so heavy that they had to be suspended from the ceiling when worn. Developed from the types of military headsets worn by high-altitude pilots, the first VR helmets enabled the user to see a virtual world superimposed over the real one. In his book of 1965, *The Ultimate Display*, Sutherland described the experience of this augmented reality:

> The ultimate display would, of course, be a room within which the
> computer can control the existence of matter. A chair displayed in such a
> room would be good enough to sit in. Handcuffs displayed in such a room
> would be confining, and a bullet displayed in such a room would be fatal.
> With appropriate programming such a display could literally be the
> Wonderland into which Alice walked.[22]

Adopting the potential of these ideas, artists and designers of the period played with the ways in which such technologies could bring about an expansion of consciousness. The Austrian architectural group Haus-Rucker Co, for example, produced a number of helmets they named 'Environmental Transformers' in 1968, individually titled 'Flyhead', 'Viewatomizer' and 'Drizzler', which would work by suppressing or enhancing certain sensorial responses, to produce an altered experience of the world (pp.92–93).

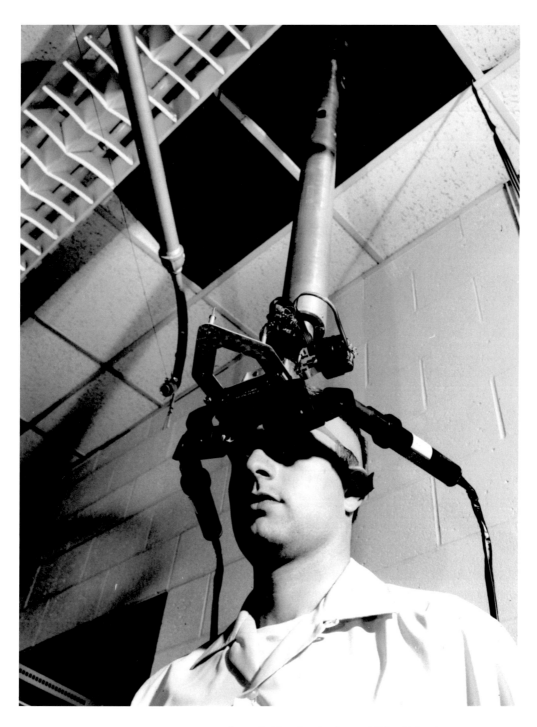

Ivan Sutherland, <u>Incredible Helmet</u>.
USA. 1968

Haus-Rucker Co (Laurids Ortner, Günter Zamp Kelp
and Klaus Pinter), photograph of the artists
wearing 'Environment Transformers', 1968

This fascination with technology did not follow the scientific rationalism of the period, but instead focused on the liberating and communicative possibilities of science. It was the psychedelic flipside of the scientific cyber-culture of the Cold War. The Environmental Transformers were portable, worn on the body, unlike the group's 'Mind Expander' seats, produced in 1967. These contraptions consisted of a double seat for a couple (made from moulded plastic, the seat was shaped so that the female member of the pair sat across the lap of the male) with an audio-visual helmet (in one version, made from inflatable plastic, in the second, a hard plastic visor) that would be lowered to encapsulate the couple together in a media-enhanced environment. This environment would stimulate the senses, producing an effect akin or complementary to a drug-induced state. In 1968 this concept was expanded to create 'Yellow Heart', an inflatable the size of a small building, housing an inflatable bed for two. The inflatable would gently pulse with light and air to create a hallucinogenic, erotic space (p.94).

Such multi-media environments had their medical and fictional parallels. Wilhelm Reich, the Austrian-American psychoanalyst (later discredited and prosecuted for 'lewd' behaviour), had proposed an electrical contraption called the 'Orgone Accumulator' in 1940, based on his erroneous belief that libidinal energy (the 'orgone') could be harnessed by a metal-lined device, in which a patient would sit to absorb its therapeutic benefits. Echoes of Reich's thoughts can also be seen in movies that proposed, in light-hearted ways, the idea of the machine as erotic stimulant, such as *Barbarella* (the 'Excessive Machine') and Woody Allen's comedy of 1973, *Sleeper* (the 'Orgasmatron').

Whereas the Haus-Rucker Co helmets suggested that technology offered some kind of escapism from the world (a process of 'switching on' in order to 'tune out'), the Polish artist Krzysztof Wodiczko suggested a similar wearable technology as a means of amplifying the world around him, which he called his 'Personal Instrument' (p.95). The work was specified for his sole use, and demonstrated in a public performance in Warsaw in 1969. By waving his gloved hands, Wodiczko could control the effects of environmental sounds. Instead of suggesting the liberating potential of technology, Wodiczko pointed to its pervasive effects. His work was deeply influenced by his experience working for the state electronics company in Warsaw as an engineer, and was a commentary on the control and surveillance activities of the state.[23]

The Austrian artist Walter Pichler, a colleague of Haus-Rucker Co, fascinated with the sensorial experience achieved through the manipulation of technology, also explored its negative connotations, in a series of works known as 'Prototypes' of 1966–9. These works, although employing the shiny-surfaced and Space Age vocabulary of the period, were nevertheless cynical commentaries on the isolating effects of modern media on human experience. Two particular works, 'TV-Helmet'

 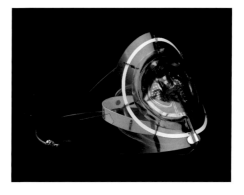

left:
Haus-Rucker Co (Laurids Ortner, Günter Zamp
Kelp and Klaus Pinter), 'Environment Transformer':
helmet with visor and mobile central disc.
Plastics, colour adhesive, metal. 1968

right:
Haus-Rucker Co (Laurids Ortner, Günter Zamp
Kelp and Klaus Pinter), 'Environment Transformer':
helmet with visor and supple membrane. Plastics
and metal. 1968

Haus-Rucker Co, Yellow Heart, inflatable structure. 1968

(also known as 'Portable Living Room') and 'Small Room', were described by Pichler as 'isolation cells',[24] in which the political potential of television, to control and mediate experience of world events, was explored (p.96). As well as the helmets, Pichler created inflatable and mobile environments (with the architect Hans Hollein), and also clothing, such as the 'Radio-Vest' (1966) and 'Standard Suit' (1968), which incorporated electronic media into clothing and explored the idea of design as a prosthetic extension of the body – the 'Finger-Stretcher' (1967), for example. By suggesting the negative and controlling effects of technologies, Pichler also returned to their Cold War sources, as Schöllhammer has pointed out, alluding to weaponry, aircraft-building and space travel in the functioning, materials and styling of the Prototypes.[25]

The Cybernetic Body

Krzysztof Wodiczko, <u>Personal Instrument</u>, with
photograph showing the object in use. 1969

right:
Walter Pichler. <u>Standard Suit</u>,
construction drawing. Pencil
and colour pencil on paper,
dry-mounted on aluminium. 1968

left:
Walter Pichler, <u>TV helmet:</u>
<u>Portable Living Room</u>. Polyester,
varnished white, integrated TV
monitor with TV cable. 1967

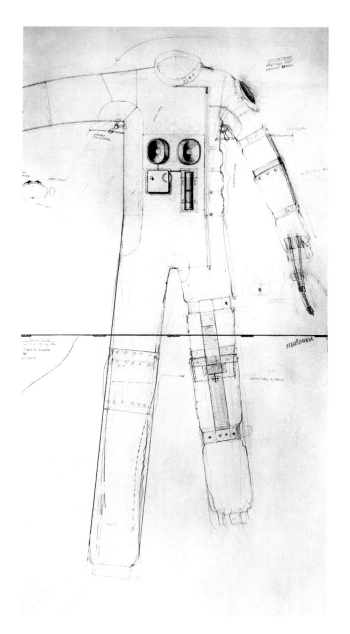

CLOTHING AS ARCHITECTURE

As previously mentioned, portable and miniaturized electronic technologies were crucial factors in the blurring of the relationship between architecture and clothing. If technologies necessary to the provision of comfortable environments, such as lighting and temperature control, could be provided by a minimum of apparatus, they could be worn on the body or carried around. Similarly, once lightweight synthetic fabrics were durable enough to be used to create architectural structures, buildings would be as simple to 'put on' as clothes. Marshall McLuhan drew a parallel between buildings and attire when he said:

> clothing, as an extension of the skin, can be seen as a heat-control mechanism and as a means of defining the self socially. In these respects, clothing and housing are near twins, though clothing is both nearer and elder; for housing extends the inner heat-control mechanisms of our organism, while clothing is a more direct extension of the outer surface of the body.[26]

In a seminal article written in 1965 entitled 'A Home Is Not a House', Reyner Banham imagined an inflatable home furnished with technologies, in which the architecture is merely an air-supported skin: 'When your house contains . . . so many services that the hardware could stand up by itself without any assistance from the house, why have a house to hold it up?'[27] Low-pressure inflatables, made from PVC, were celebrated by architects as the ultimate 'dematerialized' architecture: soft and pliable, transparent and ephemeral, they represented the extreme potential of plastics to define a new kind of space. The futuristic capacity of pneumatics was explored in films such as *Barbarella* and *The Touchables* (Robert Freeman, 1968), both of which show inflatable structures as erotic playgrounds (p.100). Banham described the sets of *Barbarella* as 'the living, breathing vision of a friendly, sexy, adaptable personal environment'.[28] Inflatables, like electronics (as we have seen earlier, p.81), were equated with sexual liberation and experimentation in the 1960s; like drugs, too, they were viewed as having mind-enhancing and perception-altering potential. In France, the radical group Utopie (formed in 1967) also proposed the inflatable as a socially and politically provocative form. In 1968 they staged an exhibition entitled *Structures gonflables* at the Musée de l'Art Moderne de la Ville in Paris, in which they showed military and engineering products alongside new architectural experiments. Through their journal, *Utopie*, they combined visionary architectural thinking with politically provocative statements and attacks on consumerism, celebrating the ephemeral and mobile character of inflatables. Quite how the inflatable served as a politically challenging form of architecture was never really clear, but it certainly served as

François Dallegret, Un-house. Transportable Standard-of-Living Package. The Environment Bubble, from Reyner Banham, 'A Home Is Not a House', Art in America (April 1965). Indian ink on translucent film and gelatin on transparent acetate

The <u>Touchables</u> directed by Robert Freeman. 1968.
An inflatable structure designed by Arthur Quarmby

an oppositional metaphor to all that was perceived as inhuman, alienating and impenetrable in traditional architectural and institutional structures.[29]

The inflatable spaces, helmets and clothing designed by Haus-Rucker Co, Pichler and also Archigram were considered by their authors as a hybrid of clothing and architecture, echoing the view of Marshall McLuhan. Discussing his inflatable structures, Pichler observed in 1997 that 'these rooms were also suits... we viewed clothing as being the first shell of architecture, clothing as the first cover and only then space'.[30] Peter Cook, a founder-member of Archigram, discussed this kind of architecture as the 'man-container' or 'environment-as-a-suit', which was a form of technological habitat ideally suited to extreme situations, such as inhospitable locations and post-disaster landscapes.[31] The main prototypes for this kind of mobile architecture were Archigram's Cushicle and Suitaloon projects. The Cushicle utilized an armature, like a set of folding limbs, to which were connected necessary communications devices, a helmet and water supply. The whole structure would be enclosed only when the outer skin was inflated. The Suitaloon of 1967, was an entirely portable version, which 'blurred the boundaries between different kinds of bodily enclosures, of buildings and clothes, of inside and outside' (p.102).[32] Habitats like the Suitaloon were mobile enclosures for one (or, occasionally, two), inflated when the user/wearer needed or wanted to 'be at home'. One Suitaloon was designed to connect its structure and services to another to form a single, shared environment. When shown at the Milan Triennale in 1968 by Michael Webb and David Greene, the Suitaloon was worn along with an 'Infogonk' or prototypical 'virtual reality' headset in order to provide the media-based environmental stimulus that might constitute a lived-in space. By connecting the wearer with a virtual world, Archigram's proposal suggested that life could be lived inside the mind, once the technologies could be provided to 'plug in', in order to 'tune out'. Another Austrian collective, Coop Himmelblau, proposed the 'White Suit' in 1969, a form of television helmet in and on which audio-visual information appears, in conjunction with smells. Tactile information is relayed through a pneumatic vest. The wearer, as Steven Harris and Deborah Berke have described, is imagined as 'a lone nomad preparing to survive in an over-crowded, polluted environment; a subject whose city/environment is so transportable it can be worn on its own body'.[33]

In 1969 the Japanese Metabolist architect Kisho Kurokawa made the declaration that 'architecture from now will increasingly take on the character of equipment'.[34] Kurokawa developed his concept of a 'capsule architecture' using the cybernetic concept of feedback:

> the capsule is a feedback mechanism in an information-oriented, a 'technetronic' society. It is a device which permits us to reject undesired information ... To protect us from the flood of information and the one-way traffic in information, we should have a feedback mechanism and a mechanism which rejects unnecessary information. The capsule serves as such a space.[35]

In other words, architecture was to become not only shelter from environmental conditions, but also a kind of filter for media and information. Architecture as equipment also suggested the portability of the futuristic habitat – a home to be

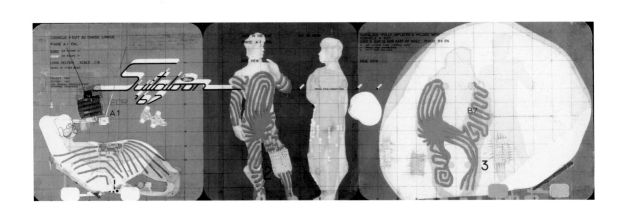

Michael Webb (Archigram), <u>Suitaloon</u>. Collage of
prints with added ink drawing, lettering and colour
film mounted on card and laminated. 1967

Coop Himmelblau and Michael Holzer(Wolf D. Prix and
Helmut Swiczinsky), drawing of Villa Rosa, M 1:20.
Black ink on tracing paper, Letraset. 1968

carried around, perhaps worn in the way that an astronaut 'wears' his necessary life-support systems in the form of an EVA suit.

In another version of how to equip the body for future living, Coop Himmelblau developed a prototype for a pneumatic living unit in 1968, called the Villa Rosa. The Villa Rosa was conceived as an environment 'supported through projections of sound, light and fragrance', and was composed of interconnecting spaces, including a 'pulsating unit with revolving bed, projection and sound program'; pneumatic units that could vary their size accordingly when inflated or deflated; and mobile units contained in a 'helmet shaped suitcase', from which 'one can inflate an air-conditioned shell, complete with bed'.[36] As a means of asserting the Villa Rosa's potential as a Space Age environment, Coop Himmelblau offered the project to NASA to be used as virtual environments for astronauts.[37]

They were not the only ones to consider the value of inflatables to Space Age research, in astronaut training and for therapeutic benefits, to understand the effects of weightlessness. A proposal of 1964 for an 'Environmental Garment Structure' was illustrated in the *Body Covering* exhibition of 1968 in New York (see p.10), but, sadly, no images of the actual prototypes exist. The structure, essentially an inflatable cocoon for the body, was described as follows:

> *[It is] ... a totally dialectical personal environmental structure for men and women. Made of extremely light gage nylon mylar laminate, the garment would cover the wearer completely. It would be slightly inflated thereby surrounding the wearer with a pocket of air, the temperature of which would be under his control ... The structure would also be equipped with vibrating devices having two basic functions. The first would be to exercise the subject's body without his having to move. The second would have a therapeutic value, as it would keep the body in a tension free state by massaging areas of the body which might become tense due to sudden anxieties. The garment would have its own miniature computer to sense and immediately alleviate these tensions. The same computer could function as a warning device against people and things which might upset the wearer, and allow him to avoid their presence.[38]*

The wearable habitats of the Space Age were intended not only to support and protect the body, but also to filter the unsettling effects of modern life. Yet, unsettling and dangerous conditions were often seen as the result of technological acceleration in a period of heightened political and social tension. Although an understanding of cybernetics offered designers and architects the means to envisage new kinds of structures with heightened technological and communicative functionality, there remained the fearful prospect that such technologies were as likely to lead to isolation, alienation and destruction as they would provide the means of liberation.

David Green, Archigram, inflatable suit-home (suit
made by Pat Haines). 1968. Suit inflated and being
occupied as a home. This is a working model for the
Suitaloon project by Michael Webb, which was made
for the Milan Triennale of 1968

EPILOGUE:

FUTURE SHOCKED

FUTURE SHOCKED

By the end of the 1960s a host of contemporary concerns about over-consumption, militarism and the environment had darkened the mood of optimism that had characterized that decade. The shiny Space Age dreaming of the mid-1960s was replaced in fashion by references to hippie and protest culture, flower power and the dress codes of festivals, marches, 'sit-ins' and 'be-ins'. Rudi Gernreich, a designer closely associated with the sexy futurology of fashion in the 1960s, reflected the shift in mood in his collection of 1970 for Harmon Knitwear. On the catwalk, he accessorized his models with guns, dressed in a version of army fatigues with dog tags and army boots. Gernreich claimed that his collection commemorated the shooting of students protesting against the war in Cambodia by the US military at Kent State University, Ohio, earlier that year, an action that had in turn provoked national student strikes and demonstrations against the government.[1] In the same year, invited to curate a show on the subject of Future Fashion for the Osaka World's Fair and also to set forward his views in *Life* magazine, Gernreich suggested a future in which fashion would 'disappear' (in his words, 'fashion will go out of fashion').[2] Gernreich's presentation for Osaka consisted of two models, their bodies and heads completely stripped of hair, who silently removed their clothes in performance until finally lying naked on the floor. Whilst adeptly using shock tactics to enliven his shows, Gernreich nevertheless realized that his futuristic predictions had to reflect the change in mood by the start of the new decade.

In 1970 Alvin Toffler, an American academic and former editor of *Fortune* magazine, published *Future Shock*, a polemical and hyperbolic account of fears about the future, which explored what he termed the 'accelerative thrust' of modern living. Toffler's fears were manifold and wide-ranging, and included rapid technological change, the loss of social cohesion and the disintegration of traditional personal relations in favour of a 'surfeit of sub-cults'. For Toffler, the post-war world had produced a 'culture of impermanence': disposability, fast-changing fashions and fads, the profusion of new media, 'experience' cultures and 'lifestyle' industries had all resulted in an 'over-stimulated' society. Although covering similar themes to 1960s counter-cultural gurus such as Marshall McLuhan and Timothy Leary[3] – new media, acceleration, social sub-cultures, cybernetic systems and, of course, sex and drugs – Toffler injected a conservative note of caution to his book. He compared the experience of the 'future-shocked' individual with that of the soldier under fire:

> *Shells burst on every side. Bullets whiz past erratically. Flares light the sky. Shouts, groans and explosions fill his ears. Circumstances change from instant to instant. To survive in such over stimulating environments, the soldier is driven to operate in the upper reaches of his adaptive range.*[4]

Rudi Gernreich, collection for Harmon Knitwear,
shown 1970. Photograph by William Claxton

According to Toffler, the pace of change in modern culture causes the 'future shock victim' to experience similar disruption:

> caught in the turbulent flow of change, called upon to make significant, rapid-fire life decisions, he feels not simply intellectual bewilderment, but disorientation at the level of personal values. As the pace of change quickens, this confusion is tinged with self-doubt, anxiety and fear.[5]

Like Christopher Booker's critique of the Swinging Sixties, *The Neophiliacs,* Toffler's book marked a sudden, disenchanted move against the freedoms and excitements of the 1960s. Both Booker and Toffler used some of the fashion codes of the decade – miniskirts, PVC boots, paper dresses – as signifiers of social decline.

Futuristic fashions also lost their sheen because the technological advances of the 1950s and '60s were increasingly regarded as having potentially catastrophic effects on the environment. A loss of faith in synthetic fabrics in the 1970s was in keeping with a widespread disaffection towards the products and consequences of a man-made world; it was also expedient given the effects of the Oil Crisis in 1973 on the stability of the petrochemical industries. Jane Schneider has termed the reaction against synthetic fabrics a form of 'sartorial reversal', which, she says, has much in common with the rejection of other forms of modernist or futuristic imaginings in the 1970s.[6] The rejection of synthetics was combined with a general disillusionment with science (and its militaristic and ecological consequences), an antagonism towards the agencies of corporatism (the multinational petrochemical corporations) and a disenchantment with the utopian rhetoric of the 1960s. By the 1970s the term 'man-made' had lost its affirmative tone, and the idea of a fast-change, throw-away product culture was under question.

Space exploration, too, was never to reach the same heights of human achievement and public fascination after the *Apollo 11* moon landing of 1969. Although the history of space exploration had had its fair shares of disasters and loss of life from the outset, the near tragedy of the *Apollo 13* mission in 1970 and the tragedy of the Soviet *Soyuz 11* mission (in which the three crew members returning from the Salyut space station were killed) tempered the mood of excitement in a Space Age future.

Cybernetic fantasies have persisted beyond the 1960s, achieving a new significance in the postmodernist discourse surrounding the body in the succeeding decades.[7] The cyborg has remained a dominant figure of dystopian projection, especially in films such as *Blade Runner* (1982) and *The Lawnmower Man* (1992), as well as in comics and animated films. Even in a post-Cold War world, some of the technologies produced in that climate of fear, exploration and competition have continued to exercise a powerful effect on the imagination, and they still, in a sense, embody our fears.

Epilogue

FEAR AND FASHION TODAY

Underlying many of the projects of the 1960s discussed in this book was an awareness that protective garments and habitats were needed to ameliorate the environmental conditions of everyday life. The anxieties of the period were not only fears about the future – of possible nuclear war or alien invasion – but also of the present – pollution, disease, a decline in the worlds' resources, too much noise, too much information. These are the worries we carry today. In fact, recently, fashion historians and commentators have turned their attention to the relationship between fear and fashion with increasing frequency. The historian Rebecca Arnold has characterized late twentieth-century fashion as the 'interplay of contradictions' in which glamour and luxury are 'counterbalanced' with a sense of ambiguity or threat:

> *The contradictory nature of fashion relates to our unease about the body and its representation, we are fascinated by and yet uncertain of the responses dress provokes: its juxtapositions can be protective, shielding the wearer from those outside their group, who are unable to read the complex signifiers that are pulled around the body. It can also expose the wearer, excavating hidden desires and fears, and unsettling the onlooker with ambivalent messages that confront taboos and challenge notions of the acceptable.*[8]

In his book *The Supermodern Wardrobe*, Andrew Bolton proposed that fashion has responded to the physical and psychological demands of contemporary experience by evolving a form of clothing with heightened functionality: affording greater protection against crime, pollution and intrusive behaviour (from surveillance cameras to crowds), and using hi-tech materials and electronics to achieve this.[9] This theme has been continued by Bradley Quinn in *Techno Fashion*, which explores the relationship between electronic and material technology and contemporary clothing.[10] Both writers assert the links between a sense of urban unease, a need for shelter and the evolution of hi-tech garments that integrate the functioning of product design. It may be that a post-9/11 culture of fear has resulted in the development of certain hybrid products that fetishize the risk element of modern living. The curator Paola Antonelli explored this territory in her exhibition *Safe: Design Takes On Risk* at the Museum of Modern Art in New York in 2006, displaying objects that 'address the spectrum of human fears and worries', ranging from environmental disaster to identity theft.[11]

Undoubtedly, designers have responded to the uncertainties of contemporary life with designs that assert the defensive potential of clothing against fearful elements. The integration of responsive and communicative technologies into garments has been proposed as a means to offset these potential threats. Recent investigations into this subject from the perspective of information technology and its impact upon the body include James E. Katz's edited collection of essays *Machines That Become Us*, which examines issues of the body, fashion and social interaction in relation to personal communications technology.[12]

In the light of these contemporary concerns, the crazy utopian predictions and chilling dystopian concerns of designers and architects during the Cold War take on a new significance. Cold War conditions produced many of the technological advancements that underpin the products of contemporary life: satellite communications and the Internet, microchips and microwave cookers, heat-resistant and bullet-proof fabrics. The arc of invention during the Cold War saw a continual stream of new processes, products and materials introduced in consumer-friendly forms to the marketplace. Not only that, but by fuelling the imagination of designers, the Cold War also had a radical effect on the ways in which fashion and design developed, leaving behind an imaginative array of fearful and hopeful visions of the future, some of which are still at play in fashion culture today.

Hans Hollein (design), Franz Hubmann (photographer),
The World is Red-White-Red: Austria glasses for
Austriennale at the Milan Triennale of 1968

Betsey Johnson (Paraphernalia, New York), White
fluorescent jacket, low belt, silver buttons, glasses
by Oliver Goldsmith. From Vogue UK, 15 April 1966.
Photograph by David Montgomery

NOTES

Introduction

[1] For an insightful discussion of the 'Iron Curtain' metaphor, see Wright (2007).

[2] Auden (1947/8).

[3] The 'atomic' references for the two-piece swimsuit are numerous: Réart, an engineer, launched his design for the two-piece swimsuit he called the bikini in the summer of 1946. A French couturier, Jacques Heim, produced a similar garment in the same year, which he called the 'atome'. Diana Vreeland, editor of American *Vogue*, described it as the most important thing since the A-bomb. See Tiffany Webber-Hanchett, 'The Bikini', in Valerie Steele (ed.), *Scribner Encyclopedia of Clothing and Fashion* (Farmington Mills, MI, 2005), vol.1, pp.155–7.

[4] Hess was a student of Tomás Maldonado at the time of his diploma project, which was published in the HfG's journal, *Ulm* (August 1967), no.19–20, pp.64–5. For a history of the school, see Lindinger (1987).

[5] Ruben Torres, quoted in Bennett-England (1967), p.94.

[6] *Body Covering* (1968), pp.26–7.

[7] Paul J. Smith, 'Introduction', *Body Covering* (1968), p.3.

[8] *Body Covering* (1968), p.20.

The Cold War Body

[1] For example, see Verity Wilson on the Mao Suit, in Steele and Major (1999); Trisha Ziff on the image of Che Guevara, Ziff (2006).

[2] Recent studies on some of these aspects of fashion in the Cold War include: Djurdja Bartlett, 'Let Them Wear Beige: The Petit-Bourgeois World of Official Socialist Dress', *Fashion Theory: Journal of Dress, Body and Culture* (June 2004), vol.8, no.2, pp.127–64; Ferenc Hammer, 'Sartorial Manoeuvres in the Dusk: Blue Jeans in Socialist Hungary', in Soper and Trentmann (2008); Stitziel (2005).

[3] In a Labour Party Conference speech of 1963, Harold Wilson described the 'new Britain' as being 'forged in the white heat of the [scientific and technological] revolution'.

[4] One such account of cultural competition is Caute (2003).

[5] For discussion of the *American National Exhibition* in Moscow of 1959, see May (1988), ch.7; Marling (1994), pp.243–83; Susan Reid, 'Our Kitchen Is Just as Good: Soviet Responses to the American National Exhibition in Moscow, 1959', in Crowley and Pavitt (2008), pp.153–61.

[6] Richard Nixon, cited in 'The Two Worlds: A Day-Long Debate', *New York Times* (25 July 1959), p.1.

[7] Karel Langer, 'O českou módu', *Tvar* (1948), no.4, pp.81–4; quoted in

Hlaváčková (2000), p.37.

[8] J. Spalová, 'Elegantní nebo príjemný', *Žena a móda* (1949), no.12, p.19; quoted in Hlaváčková (2000), p.39.

[9] The term 'Thaw' was used by Ilya Ehrenberg to describe the Eastern bloc situation in the mid-1950s in his novel of 1954, *The Thaw*. For discussion of the effects of the thaw on design, see Susan E. Reid, 'Design, Stalin and the Thaw', *Journal of Design History* (1997), vol.10, no.2; Reid and Crowley (2000); David Crowley, 'Thaw Modern: Design in Eastern Europe after 1956', in Crowley and Pavitt (2008), pp.129–53.

[10] For example, see Judd Stitziel, 'On the Seam between Socialism and Capitalism: East German Fashion Shows', in Crew (2003), pp.51–86.

[11] Bartlett, 'Let Them Wear Beige'.

[12] For an account of competition with the West, see Stitziel in Crew (2003).

[13] See *Life* magazine (10 August 1959). The *Life* cover image is also discussed by Beatrix Colomina, 'Enclosed by Images', in Colomina (2007), p.244.

[14] Murray Ilson, 'Style Show SRO at Soviet Exhibit', *New York Times* (2 July 1959).

[15] For a discussion of the Dior show, see Crowley, 'Thaw Modern', in Crowley and Pavitt (2008), pp.144–5; also Larissa Zakharova, 'Dior in Moscow: A Taste for Luxury in Soviet Fashion under Khrushchev', in David Crowley and Susan E. Reid (eds), *Pleasures in Socialism: Leisure and Luxury in the Eastern Bloc* (forthcoming).

[16] Daniels (2007), p.341.

[17] Cecil Lubell, 'The Materials', in *Body Covering* (1968), p. 5.

[18] The term 'military-industrial complex' was employed by President Eisenhower in his Farewell to the Nation speech of 1961, to refer to the relationship between the armed forces, private industry and political interest.

[19] Ndiaye (2006).

[20] David Riesman, 'The Nylon War', in Riesman (1964), pp.65–77.

[21] Eli Rubin, 'The Order of Substitutes: Plastic Consumer Goods in the Volkswirtschaft and Everyday Domestic Life in the GDR', in Crew (2003), pp.87–120.

[22] Ibid., p.94.

[23] Hlaváčková (2000), pp.100–01.

[24] Rubin, in Crew (2003), p.91.

[25] Jeffrey Meikle, 'Into the Fourth Kingdom: Representations of Plastic Materials, 1920–1950', *Journal of Design History* (1992), vol.5, no.3, p.179.

[26] Packard's previous books included *The Hidden Persuaders* (1957), focused on the advertising world, and *The Status Seekers* (1959), about American consumer behaviours.

[27] Reyner Banham, 'Who Is This "Pop"?', *Motif* (Winter 1962–3); reprinted in Banham (1981), pp.94–6.

[28] Sadler (2005).

[29] *Chicago Tribune* (25 October 1959).

[30] 'In Defense of Waste', *Time* magazine (18 November 1966).

[31] Kamitsis (1996), p.72.

[32] The paper dresses campaign featured in *Junge Welt* (3 May 1968), p.12. I am grateful to Dorit Lücke, formerly of the Archivarin Modesammlung, Stiftung Stadtmuseum, Berlin, for information on this subject.

[33] Hlaváčková (2000), p.90.

[34] Toffler (1970) p.54.

[35] Ibid.

The Space Age Body

[1] The National Aeronautics and Space Act of 1958 announced the founding of the National Aeronautics and Space Council (later NASA, the National Aeronautics and Space Agency). In a speech broadcast on television on 25 May 1961, President Kennedy announced the programme to put a man in space.

[2] Garn et al. (2007).

[3] Lee (2005), p.45.

[4] American *Vogue* (1 February 1939).

[5] In fact, the construction of the house on site was only a mock-up of a plastic house, using plywood, plaster and paint to simulate its plastic shell. See Beatrix Colomina, 'Unbreathed Air', in Colomina (2007), p.200.

[6] Ibid., pp.227–30.

[7] Laver was the author of several essays that discussed the social and cultural directions that dress might take in the future, such as *A Letter to a Girl on the Future of Clothes* (1946) and *The Past and Future of Clothes* (1958).

[8] Press statements made at the time by Teddy Tinling, quoted by Helena Mattsson in an unpublished research paper, www.nap.no/Forskerutdanning /Konferanse/Papers/Mattsson.doc

[9] Description of designs by Gera Wernitz for Telecafé uniforms, 18 November 1968. Courtesy of the Deutsches Modeinstitut, Berlin.

[10] Booker (1969), p.274.

[11] Valerie Steele, 'Fashion, Yesterday, Today and Tomorrow', in White and Griffiths (2000), p.11.

[12] Ibid.

[13] André Courrèges, interviewed by Betty Werther in 'Is Fashion an Art?', *Metropolitan Museum of Art Bulletin* (November 1967), vol.26, no.3, p.139.

[14] The discrepancy over who produced the first mini – either Courrèges or Quant – has been much discussed. See, for example, Steele, in White and Griffiths (2000), p.10.

[15] Courrèges, interviewed by Werther in 'Is Fashion an Art?', p.138.

[16] Quoted in Längle (2005), p.13.

[17] Lee (2005), p.28.

[18] Paco Rabanne in *Marie Claire* (1967); quoted in Kamitsis (1999), p.11.

[19] See Antoine Stinco, 'Boredom, School, Utopie', in Dessauce (1999), p.69.

[20] Ibid., p.71.

21 Quoted in Kamitsis (1996), p.56.

22 Ibid., p.72.

23 Paco Rabanne, quoted in ibid., p.68.

24 Claxton and Moffitt (1991), pp.20–21.

25 The first of these performances was staged as part of the *Edelsmeden (Jewellery)* 3 exhibition, Stedelijk Museum, Amsterdam, 1967. The second was entitled *Clothing Suggestions / Kleding Suggesties*, held on 31 January 1970 at the Art + Project Gallery, Amsterdam. For a discussion of this work, see Joris (2005).

26 Quoted from the film in Klein (1994), pp.153–4.

27 Artist's Statement, in *Sculpture to Wear* (1967).

28 P. Reyner Banham, 'The Great Gizmo, Industrial Design' (September 1965); in Banham (1981), p.108.

29 Quinn (2002), p.6.

30 Georges Teyssot, 'Hybrid Architecture: An Environment for the Prosthetic Body', *Convergence: The International Journal of Research into New Media Technologies* (2005), vol.11, no.4, pp.72–84. See also Teyssot, 'Body Building: Towards a New Organicism', *Lotus International* [Milan] (September 1997), no.94, pp.116–31.

31 Deane Simpson, 'The Vostok Cosmonauts: Training the New Soviet Person', in Zukowsky (2001), pp.108–13.

32 Hans Hollein, in 'Alles ist Architektur', *Bau: Schrift für Architektur und Städtebau* (April 1968), vol.23, no.1–2.

33 Manfred E. Clynes and Nathan S. Kline, 'Cyborgs and Space', in *Astronautics* (September 1960); reprinted in Gray (1995), p.29.

The Cybernetic Body

1 Mary Wollstonecraft Shelley's novel *Frankenstein: The Modern Prometheus* was first published anonymously in 1818, then under her name in 1831. For a discussion of the image of science in cinema, see Frayling, 2006.

2 Alwin Nikolais in *Body Covering* (1968), p.42.

3 Diana Dew, 'Turn On, Turn Off', *Time* magazine (20 January 1967).

4 For a detailed analysis of these tendencies and attitudes, see Cook (1970).

5 Manfred E. Clynes and Nathan S. Kline, 'Cyborgs and Space', in *Astronautics* (September 1960); reprinted in Gray (1995), p.29.

6 *The Soft Machine* was first published in Paris in 1961 and then by the radical Grove Press in the USA in 1966.

7 Peter Galison, 'The Ontology of the Enemy: Norbert Wiener and the Cybernetic Vision', *Critical Inquiry* (Autumn 1994), vol.21, no.2, pp.228–66.

8 Georg Schöllhammer, 'The Bolted Gesture', in Breitwieser (1998), p.52.

9 For a discussion of the All-Action Office, see Branden Hookway, 'Cockpit', in Colomina, Brennan and Kim (2004), pp.22–54.

10 Time and motion studies on workplace behaviours were popular in the 1950s for the improvement of industrial efficiency, and had devel-

oped from the principles of scientific management developed by Frederick
Winslow Taylor in the 1920s.

[11] Wiener (1948); Wiener (1950).

[12] Films such as Jean-Luc Godard's *Alphaville* (1965) and Joseph Sargent's
Colossus: The Forbin Project (1970). For a discussion of this, see Crowley and
Pavitt (2008), p.168.

[13] Marshall McLuhan, *Understanding Media* (London, 1967). For
a discussion of this, see Aquin (2003), pp.13–17.

[14] Marshall McLuhan, interviewed in *Playboy* (March 1969).

[15] Stephen Willats interviewed by Christabel Stewart for SHOWstudio (n.d.),
www.showstudio.com/projects/multiclothing/start.html

[16] Ashby (1956); Ashby (1960).

[17] *Václav Cigler* (2003).

[18] For a discussion of avant-garde tendencies in Czech art and design in the
1960s, see Havránek (1999).

[19] Schöllhammer, in Breitwieser (1998), p.50.

[20] See Rheingold (1985); Rheingold (1991).

[21] *Chicago Tribune* (27 November 1960).

[22] Ivan Sutherland published this as a research paper in 1965, entitled:
'The Ultimate Display', *Proceedings of IFIP* (1965), vol.2, pp.506–8.

[23] Łukasz Ronduda, 'Krzysztof Wodiczko – projektowanie i sztuka', *Piktogram*
(2007), no.7, pp.12–27. See also Crowley and Pavitt (2008), pp.181–3.

[24] A conversation with Walter Pichler, conducted and edited by Sabine
Breitwieser, in Pichler (1998), p.28.

[25] Schöllhammer, in Breitwieser (1998), p.55.

[26] McLuhan (1967/1994), pp.119–20; quoted in Quinn (2002), p.13.

[27] Reyner Banham, 'A Home Is Not a House', *Art in America* (April 1965), vol.2,
pp.70–79.

[28] Reyner Banham, 'Triumph of Software', *New Society* (31 October 1968);
reprinted in Banham (1981), pp.133–6.

[29] For a discussion of this, see Rosalie Genevro, 'Introduction', in Dessauce
(1999), pp.7–9.

[30] Breitwieser (1998), p.32.

[31] Cook (1970).

[32] Hadas Steiner, 'The Forces of Matter', *Journal of Architecture* (2005), vol.10,
no.1, pp.103–4.

[33] Quoted in Harris and Berke (1997), p.205.

[34] Kurokawa (1977), pp.26–7.

[35] Ibid., p.82.

[36] Kandeler-Fritsch and Kramer (2005), p.76.

[37] See Jana Scholze, 'Architecture or Revolution? Vienna's 1968',
in Crowley and Pavitt (2008), p.243.

[38] *Body Covering* (1968), p.41.

Epilogue

[1] On 4 May 1970 at Kent State University, Ohio, the National Guard fired on protestors during a rally against the American invasion of Cambodia. Four were killed and nine others wounded, which precipitated national protests and student strikes across America.

[2] Gernreich, quoted in Claxton and Moffitt (1991), p.27.

[3] Leary was a psychiatrist who experimented with psychedelic drugs in the 1960s, as described in his book (co-written with Richard Alpert and Ralph Metzner), *The Psychedelic Experience: A Manual Based on the Tibetan Book of the Dead* (1964).

[4] Toffler (1970), p.347.

[5] Ibid., p.344.

[6] Jane Schneider, 'In and Out of Polyester: Desire, Disdain and Global Fibre Competition', *Anthropology Today* (August 1994), vol.10, no.4, p.5.

[7] There is a broad literature on this subject, including Hayles (1999), Haraway (1991) and Bukatman (1993).

[8] Arnold (2001), p.125.

[9] Bolton (2002).

[10] Quinn (2002).

[11] Antonelli (2005).

[12] Katz (2006).

FURTHER READING

Abramov, I.P., and Ingemar Skoog, A., *Russian Spacesuits* (Chichester, 2003)

Antonelli, P., *Safe: Design Takes on Risk* (Museum of Modern Art, New York, exhib. cat., 2005)

Aquin, S. (ed.), *Global Village: The 1960s* (Montreal Museum of Fine Arts, exhib. cat., 2003)

Arnold, R., *Fashion, Desire and Anxiety: Image and Morality in the 20th Century* (New Brunswick, NJ, and London, 2001)

Ashby, W.R., *Introduction to Cybernetics* (London, 1956)

Ashby, W.R., *Design for a Brain: The Origin of Adaptive Behaviour* (London, 1960)

Auden, W.H, *The Age of Anxiety: A Baroque Eclogue* (New York, 1947; London, 1948)

Banham, P.R., *Design by Choice: Ideas in Architecture*, ed. Penny Sparke (London, 1981)

Bennett-England, R., *Dress Optional: The Revolution in Menswear* (London, 1967)

Body Covering (Museum of Contemporary Crafts, New York, exhib. cat., 1968)

Bolton, A., *The Supermodern Wardrobe* (London, 2002)

Booker, C., *The Neophiliacs: The Revolution in English Life in the Fifties and Sixties* (London, 1969)

Breitwieser, S. (ed.), *Pichler: Prototypes 1966–69* (Vienna, 1998)

Breward, C., Gilbert, D., and Lister, J. (eds), *Swinging Sixties: Fashion in London and Beyond 1955–1970* (London, 2006)

Bukatman, S., *Terminal Identity: The Virtual Subject in Postmodern Science Fiction* (Durham, NC, 1993)

Caute, D., *The Dancer Defects: The Struggle for Cultural Supremacy during the Cold War* (Oxford and New York, 2003)

Claxton, W., and Moffitt, P., *The Rudi Gernreich Book* (Cologne and London, 1991)

Colomina, B., *Domesticity at War* (Cambridge, MA, 2007)

Colomina, B., Brennan, A.M., and Kim, J. (eds), *Cold War Hothouses: Inventing Postwar Culture, from Cockpit to Playboy* (New York, 2004)

Cook, P., *Experimental Architecture* (London, 1970)

Crew, D.F. (ed.), *Consuming Germany in the Cold War* (Oxford and New York, 2003)

Crowley, D., and Pavitt, J. (eds), *Cold War Modern: Design 1945–75* (London, 2008)

Daniels, R.V., *The Rise and Fall of Communism in Russia* (New Haven, CT, 2007)

Dessauce, M., *The Inflatable Moment: Pneumatics and Protest 1968* (New York, 1999)

Dormer, P., and Turner, R., *The New Jewelry: Trends + Traditions* (London, 1985)

Frayling, C., *Mad, Bad and Dangerous? The Scientist and the Cinema* (London, 2006)

Garn, A., et al., *Exit to Tomorrow: World's Fair Architecture, Design, Fashion 1933–2005* (New York, 2007)

Gray, C.H. (ed.), *The Cyborg Handbook* (London, 1995)

Grunenberg, C. (ed.), *Summer of Love: Art of the Psychedelic Era* (London, 2005)

Guillaume, V., *Courrèges* (London, 1998)

Haraway, D.J., *Simians, Cyborgs and Women: The Reinvention of Nature* (London, 1991)

Harris, S., and Berke, D., *Architecture of the Everyday* (New York, 1997)

Havránek, V. (ed.), *Akce, slovo, pohyb, prostor: experimenty v umění šedesátých let / Action, Word, Movement, Space: Experimental Art of the Sixties* (City Gallery, Prague, exhib. cat., 1999)

Hayles, N.K., *How We Became Posthuman: Virtual Bodies in Cybernetics* (Chicago, 1999)

Hlaváčková, K., *Czech Fashion 1940–1970: Mirror of the Times* (Prague, 2000)

Jackson, L., *The Sixties: Decade of Design Revolution* (London, 1998)

Joris, Y. (ed), *Gebroken Lijnen / Broken Lines: Emmy van Leersum 1930–1984* (Ghent, 1993)

Joris, Y. (ed), *Gijs Bakker and Jewellery* (Stedelijk Museum, 's-Hertogenbosch, exhib. cat., 2005)

Kamitsis, L., *Paco Rabanne: A Feeling for Research* (Paris, 1996)

Kamitsis, L., *Paco Rabanne* (London, 1999)

Kandeler-Fritsch, M., and Kramer, T. (eds), *Get Off My Cloud: Wolf D. Prix, Coop Himmelb(l)au, Texts 1968–2005* (Ostfildern-Ruit, 2005)

Katz, J.E., *Machines That Become Us: The Social Context of Personal Communication Technology* (New Brunswick, NJ, and London, 2006)

Klein, W., *In and Out of Fashion*, ed. Mark Holborn (London, 1994)

Kurokawa, K., *Metabolism in Architecture* (London, 1977)

Längle, E., *Pierre Cardin: Fifty Years of Fashion and Design* (London, 2005)

Laver, J., *A Letter to a Girl on the Future of Clothes* (London, 1946)

Laver, J., *The Past and Future of Clothes* (London, 1958)

Leary, T., Alpert, R., and Metzner, R., *The Psychedelic Experience: A Manual Based on the Tibetan Book of the Dead* (New Hyde Park, NY, 1964)

Lee, S., *Fashioning the Future: Tomorrow's Wardrobe* (London, 2005)

Lindinger, H. (ed.), *Ulm: die Moral der Gegestände* (Bauhaus Archive, Berlin, Centre Pompidou, Paris, and Wilhelm Ernst & Sohn, Berlin, exhib. cat., 1987)

Marling, K.A., *As Seen on TV: The Visual Culture of Everyday Life in the 1950s* (Cambridge, MA, 1994)

May, E.T., *Homeward Bound: American Families in the Cold War Era* (New York, 1988)

McLuhan, M., *Understanding Media: The Extension of Man* (London 1967; reprinted 1994)

Ndiaye, P.A., *Nylon and Bombs: Dupont and the March of Modern America*, trans. E. Forster (Baltimore, MD, 2006)

Paco Rabanne (Musée de la Mode, Marseille, exhib. cat., 1995)

Quinn, B., *Techno Fashion* (Oxford and New York, 2002)

Reid, S.E., and Crowley, D. (eds), *Style and Socialism* (Oxford and New York, 2000)

Rheingold, H., *Tools for Thought: The People and Ideas behind the Next Computer Revolution* (New York, 1985)

Rheingold, H., *Virtual Reality* (New York, 1991)

Riesman, D., *Abundance for What? And Other Essays* (New York, 1964)

Rubitzsch, G., *Off the Wall: Fashion from East Germany 1964 to 1980* (New York, 2005)

Sadler, S., *Archigram: Architecture without Architecture* (Cambridge, MA, 2005)

Sculpture to Wear: Gijs Bakker and Emmy Van Leersum (Ewan Phillips Gallery, London, exhib. cat., 1967)

Soper, K., and Trentmann, F. (eds), *Citizenship and Consumption* (Basingstoke, 2008)

Steele, V., and Major, J.S. (eds), *China Chic* (New Haven, CT, and London, 1999)

Stitziel, J., *Fashioning Socialism: Clothing, Politics and Consumer Culture in East Germany* (Oxford, 2005)

Toffler, A., *Future Shock* (London, 1970)

Topham, S., *Where's My Space Age?* (Munich and London, 2003)

Turner, R., *Contemporary Jewelry: A Critical Assessment 1945–75* (London, 1976)

Turner, R., *Jewelry in Europe and America: New Times, New Thinking* (London, 1996)

Václav Cigler: A Absolventi Oddelenia Sklo V Architectúre na Vysokéj škole výtvarných umění v Bratislavě 1965–1979 (Galerie Pokorná, Prague, and Slovenská Národná Galéria, Bratislava, exhib. cat., 2003)

White, N., and Griffiths, I. (eds), *The Fashion Business: Theory, Practice, Image* (Oxford, 2000)

Wiener, N., *Cybernetics; or, Control and Communication in the Animal and the Machine* (Cambridge, MA, 1948)

Wiener, N., *The Human Use of Human Beings: Cybernetics and Society* (Boston, MA, 1950)

Wright, P., *Iron Curtain: From Stage to Cold War* (Oxford, 2007)

Ziff, T., *Che Guevara: Revolutionary and Icon* (London, 2006)

Zijl, I. van, *Gijs Bakker: Objects to Use*, trans. J. Kirkpatrick (Rotterdam, 2000)

Zukowsky, J. (ed.), *2001: Building for Space Travel* (Chicago and New York, 2001)

IMAGE CREDITS

Roger-Viollet / Topfoto: 28

© Ronald Nameth, 1966-2006. All Rights Reserved: 78

© SODRAC, Montreal and DACS, London 2008 / Coll. François Dallegret,
    Montréal: 99

© 20th Century Fox. BFI Stills Collection: 100

United States Information Agency: 27

UPM Museum of Decorative Arts Prague: 18 (Photo: Gabriel Urbánek), 24, 31, 35

© V&A Images: Front cover, 6, 9, 37 (left and right), 40, 50, 63 (left and right),
    66, 86, 87 (left, top right, bottom right), 107

Warner Bros. Entertainment Inc. Clip and Still Licensing / Photofest / Hardy
    Amies Archive: 46

ACKNOWLEDGEMENTS

I wish to extend my gratitude to Maria Mileeva for her sterling work on the
preparation of this book. Thanks are also due to V&A colleagues Frances Ambler,
Christopher Breward, Ruth Cribb, Mark Eastment, Charlotte King, Jana Scholze,
Sarah Sonner, Sonnet Stanfill, Eva White, Claire Wilson and to David Crowley,
my co-curator on Cold War Modern. Emma and Kirsty from APFEL produced
a beautiful book design, and Delia Gaze was a scrupulous editor. This book
is for Hugh, Clare and Hilary, for their sartorial advice over the years.

INDEX

*page numbers in italics
refer to illustrations*